MUM, FIND LOVE AGAIN

MUM, FIND LOVE AGAIN

Shame, Self-Love- Identity

MUM, FIND LOVE AGAIN

SHAME | SELF-LOVE | IDENTITY

IZIN AKIOYA

Dedication

For Lili, the love of my life.

You have my permission, you didn't need anyone's,
But just in case you thought you did, you have mine, completely,
To love and to be loved, just as you are.
Let me be your accomplice in the love story of your dreams.

Contents

Introduction

This conflicted identity, the struggle with my place in the light of my family's social standing was the identity that I took into adulthood. Constantly dogged by Christian doctrine on pre-marital sex combined with the commonplace cultural repression of my sexuality, scarred by sexual brutality, I had no tolerance for anyone's sexual gratification at my expense, to the degree that I questioned my sexuality. I took no joy in sex, yet, I had a growing appetite for it.

It took almost four years of trying, to finally get this book written. I only made significant headway when I had the gumption to learn how to write and then to research broadly, in answer to my lingering questions in ensuring that I present authentic, yet informed perspectives. I think I was also held back by my fear of this book. Fear of what I would then look like and be thought of by the people who read it. They will know who I am. From the moment it publishes, there will be no turning back. Like everything that I've attempted to do, I had been stuck on the need to do it just right, forgetting that excellence is often discovered in the doing. Despite these initial challenges, I look back with thanks for the journey. Those years set the context for the book you are about to read. They sharpened my observational skills, clarified my perspective, and reaffirmed my obsession to share this perspective on identity, love, and attainment.

I have come to revere the value of aloneness, of solitude that allows internal dialogue, permitting one to hear words and meanings that are often lost in the company of others. Failing at romance, and then choosing not to use it as a remedy for boredom has meant that I've had alone time; time that allowed me to be present in my mother's life, in a way that is hardly possible when one juggles a career, marriage, and family. Because of my single status, I have had the opportunity to *see Lili* again and again in my mature years, years when I've built perspectives. Years when I've had the opportunity to explore people, culture, and doctrine on my own, with my own eyes. These years have been crucial to how I have understood and interpreted her story, and how I am now attempting to tell it.

Every time I visited or moved in with my family, after time apart or living elsewhere or away for work, I landed on something – an emotion, a bias, just something – that would make me pause and wonder: why does Lili act in this manner? why does she believe in this or that? Those moments were the lights that forged this book, the aha! moments. They gave me keen insight into her fundamentals; for that, I am deeply thankful.

I may never know when Lili decided she was no longer permitted to love herself or to be loved by anyone. It may have occurred somewhere around age 19 when she became the wife to a wealthy older man, or in her 20s when they separated. Sometimes, I think that her self-deprecating tendencies started with her closer involvement with the church. That definitely preceded comments about her status; it brought with it many *if only* moments, "If only your father had honoured his word, if only I hadn't married him," and so on. Those were the years of hard discrimination; the years when my father's absence rankled and filled me with hopelessness.

Lili had been a star dancer and athlete in her secondary school days, the life of the party, dating her medical doctor-to-be boyfriend – one of many suitors. Things took a different turn when she was *noticed* by my father, a well-known, well-connected, money man. In a short time, introductions were made, and at age 19, she was married to a man about two decades older, with children close to her age. Lili rarely tells the story of the boyfriend arriving from Lagos, finding that she was married, and the dramatic tears that ensued. I do not know if those years were the beginning of her unhappiness, I am however certain that they signalled her first trauma, one she has likely never resolved.

Marriage as a young wife to a wealthy patriarch did not deliver on the promise of a better life and tertiary education. As other women followed (in concubine and co-wife), so were days filled with chores, caregiving, and occasional coitus with the big man upstairs, who had his other wives living on the ground floor while he and the poster wife resided on the top floor section of his big white house. It is little wonder that she found the gumption to leave that marriage, despite the lack of opportunity she would later contend with.

In the years since, I have hardly seen her choose anything other than self-denial, some of it based on the classic hardship of a single income family, a good part of it based on a shrinking and bowing that she has carried through every sphere of her life. Self-denial which I believe is an outcome of shame robbed her of many freedoms and happiness that were likely within her reach. I wish she didn't spend those years in penance. My siblings and I never asked for it and when I look back, I see the root of my self-limiting behaviour in my mother's shame.

In a lot of ways, she is still in penance to a belief system that remains at the foundation of her identity. For her and many other women raised in my society, social acceptance is a big part of personal identity, social acceptance is identity. It means love, it means value and worth captured in specific attainments and statuses, and it is nearly impossible to be happy without the stamp of approval and honour that those statuses bestow. For women born in her time, having lost their honour or acceptance defined by specific labels, it is almost impossible to make a fresh start at a life filled with self-love at no one's behest.

Lili's years of self-despise were definitely in tune with her own beliefs about right and wrong, and what is honourable and what isn't. But that was not all that it hinged on. There were, and still are, labels and stereotypes that I see her struggle with. To a good degree, her inability to simply breathe is coloured by the misadventure of an inner religious and social circle that reinforces her convictions.

I write for Lili, but I also write for my slightly-over-30 divorced friend, Iretiogo. I write for people the world over, who do not fit stereotypes and expectations and have found themselves unlovable, excluded, or abused. I write for those who have inadvertently internalised shame culture and biases, judging themselves and others by them. I hope that they will find a voice through this book, that they will break free of the burdens of martyrdom and penance to which they owed no one. I hope that those who judge will come to a better understanding of biases, their roots, collectives, and humanity. In the later portions of this book, I show the connection between culture, self-concept, and life attainment, share conscious life practices, provide growth tools, and guidance on arriving at personal identity – a journey that must be taken in solitude, yet in the company of many.

Sometimes, the witness is a bigger victim than the actual victim. Sharing my perspectives in this book has strengthened me, taking me on a journey of discovery. My hope is that the lessons in it empower people *to live a million lifetimes, yet one, to advance without resistance.*

Chapter 1

Living with Shame

When asked about my father, before his death, responses indicating my parents' separation were often met with an uncomfortable silence, followed by more questions – is your mum the only wife? and when I responded no, the usual follow-up question was – is she the first wife? and when I answered in the negative again, I got an uncomfortable *okay* that I soon became accustomed to. In my teenage years, I would usually leave the conversation at that. I didn't fully understand what was wrong, I just knew that my family status was flawed by the responses that I received. That mostly negative sentiment changed to empathy when my father died. I no longer had to speak of my parents' separation, I had simply lost a parent, and new respectability was ascribed to my family in tone, mannerisms, and shared sadness that we often exhibit when we hear of the passing of a parent or relative. There were no negative connotations; the conversations did not spiral into uncomfortable territory. This new *story* gave me in my adult years distance from the feeling that my family was not the ideal. What it didn't give me was the opportunity to say that *it hadn't mattered all along; my mother and family had always been respectable.*

Years later, my encounters with blended families outside Nigeria where siblings are introduced exactly as they are – without uncomfortable and fidgety faces, loud silences, interjections of *hmmmns* and *haaaas*, or the scintillated ears wide open expressions caused me to realise that I had internalised biases about family status and that my responses were in tandem. Subconsciously, we reject what we see others reject. When spurned, we are first surprised, even hurt, then, depending on our prevailing worldview, we soon find ourselves towing a line we do not actively choose. In extreme cases, we turn around to become the custodians of behaviours that we suffered in our pasts.

Shame culture is a primary enabler of women's stigmatisation and self-limiting behaviour. It may be touched on when issues around gender roles are raised, yet, it is submerged by bigger themes, and understandably so; the big issues are many, urgent, and easier to address. These include political participation, education, child marriage, equitable pay, and economic security. Not often enough are moral norms in shaming cultures considered on their own; as an advocacy concern, as a basis for women's quality of life and attainment. This is understandable when you consider the fact that shame culture relies on religious doctrines and age-long rules of behaviour. Doctrines are sacred, we find it hard to scrutinise them despite the enthusiasm that we bring to thinking critically about other aspects of life. A vast majority of us, myself included, are simply averse to raising any questions on moral codes. Unfortunately, doctrines hold historical references and stories that we adopt as the foundations of good and bad, right and wrong. They allot labels and we embrace those labels because *doctrine is sacred*. In the Christian religion, for example, the widow may be shown mercy, the sinner may be forgiven, the ideal is exalted, and so on. It is complex to attempt to untangle the role of shame from society to society and to determine where to draw the line between dated rules of conduct and real-world scenarios when everyone is coloured by his or her own life experiences.

How does one advocate against shame? How does one categorise and define the role of shame in women's attainment without coming across as biased or frivolous? How does one say that shame is gendered and that gendered shame limits women's agency and opportunities? What does advocacy around shame do for humanity? How do we straddle the marriage between inclusiveness and social boundaries in a manner that ensures ethical behaviour? These are the questions that I hope to explore in the first few chapters of this book.

Anyone familiar with day-to-day living in Africa can allude to women's shaming as a commonplace way of life. In families with fertility challenges, women are quickly branded. The prevalence of female genital mutilation in the region and the lack of urgency in response to rape is coloured by a shaming that shadows women at every stage of life. A rape victim and her family might be more interested in maintaining the perception of her sexual purity than in seeking justice. Parenting women will resort to desperate extremes to hide their children's failure or inadequacies due to the direct impact on their reputations. This situation may not be better globally.

Erika Sanchez, an American poet, and writer wrote:

> *Single mothers are frequently used as a case study for society's many ills, with many politicians quick to blame this*

> *vulnerable group of people. Presidential candidate Sen. Rand Paul, R-Ky., for instance, blamed the protests in Baltimore on 'the breakdown of the family structure, the lack of fathers, the lack of sort of a moral code in our society.' On the 50th anniversary of the war on poverty, Rep. Louie Gohmert, R-Texas, made a speech suggesting single mothers were abusing welfare programs. According to him, in the 1960s the federal government enabled these women's undesirable behavior by providing them financial support. Former Rep. Michele Bachmann, R-Minn., recently condemned single mothers for 'the decay of the American family' and has blamed the government for encouraging women to have children out of wedlock, which perpetuates poverty. Former Sen. Rick Santorum, R-Pa., another presidential candidate, said that single moms are 'breeding more criminals' and are ruining the country.*

Erika Sanchez, 2015

In Nigeria, (the country where I come from) even the staunchly averse express little concern for male morality and sexual discipline. What is often communicated is an aversion to women's sexuality. In this mixed culture where I was raised, where Christian monogamy and Islamic polygamy reside side by side, both the polygamist man with several wives and/or concubines and his first wife – by virtue of her being the *first* – are of respectable status. The women who come after are another story. It doesn't matter the way they surface, what matters is the deeply ingrained bias about them. This bias remains as fiercely ingrained as the underlying belief *that African men are naturally polygamous*. It is quite complex, filled with assumptions of irresponsibility, inappropriateness, greed, disgrace and disloyalty, etc. The choice adjectives ascribed range from mild tags like foolish and unwise to serious indictments like a home breaker, greedy, money-chasing woman who will do anything to be part of a wealthy establishment, even in circumstances where there is no wealth to be amassed. The mental stance towards it seeks to confirm what it has already assumed, hardly interested in the details.

There is mockery and shaming that is simply allotted to the *other woman*. The same shame is associated with single parenting women, women who have married more than once, despite the implicit permission to indulge in multiple sexual liaisons before and during the marriage which is granted to men – permission that often translates into a litany of sexual partners, and children out of wedlock. The need, no obsession to save face, seems to be a feminine burden alone.

In a lot of ways, what we live by in this part of the world is a doctrine of Christian and Islamic morals steeped in an *African honour-shame ideology* that is ahead of both faiths. To different degrees, many cities across Nigeria, and more broadly Africa, reflect this mix. Patriarchy remains entrenched and the transition from polygamous to monogamous lifestyles has retained a shaming sub-culture that is anchored on power dynamics. Status and attainment are defined by family and community association. What *A* does results in how *A's* family is perceived. Defaulting from the expected ways may result in censure from one's inner circle. Yet, rules of culture do not apply to all. One story will differ from the other based on who tells it, whose father or mother is the money man, and what the money man can do to keep a story from becoming one's demise in society. The *victim* may not often be the *victim*; the *victor* may not often be the *survivor*. As the money man rules so it is done. So, culture becomes a tool of shame and yet a tool of power; it panders to money, status, and the who is who.

In cultures where shaming is a common outcome of noncompliance with the moral code of conduct, it is often effected along gender lines. In the case of single parents, without the knowledge of the circumstances leading to an *unconventional status*, women are branded. On the other hand, across all sub-groups in Nigeria, divorced and/or single parenting men are excused from any demands of martyrdom and penance. The majority are offered support in the form of a new wife (and in some cases, new wives) or caregivers to ease their burden and take care of them and their children. While many divorced males find it quite easy to marry any woman of their choice at their discretion, the case is hardly the same for divorced women who may be excluded, and/or advised to remain single – embrace piety to retain some level of respectability.

In cases where single parenting women have re-married, many have been obligated to leave their children to be raised by grandparents and extended family, to *commence new beginnings* without the baggage of children. In reality, what this means is that the new husband would not be comfortable in the company of children by another man. While women marrying men with children are expected to *naturally adopt and nurture*, the opposite is the case for women. In the same vein, it is common practice to exclude such women from the dating pool for single men. A single man dating a woman with a child or children just does not look good in Nigeria, it just doesn't. These acts of segregation are perpetuated by men and women alike to date.

Single-mother shaming in Nigeria links closely with a moral system that is uncomfortable with women's sexual participation and expression. Slut slurs and prejudices are anchored on the belief that women should be presented to marriage in *pure form* – and I use that word, *presented,* deliberately. There is a prevailing sense that even if women had been sexually liberated before marriage, there must be no physical evidence of their indulgence. This thinking is communicated in households from the moment a girl begins to assimilate. Conversely, this addiction to the purity of the single woman makes an about-turn at the sight of a woman who was previously married.

In a society where the dating game panders to the single woman's desire to find a husband, for the woman who was married with kids, it morphs into something even more sinister. She who has had children has no *real* honour, she who has no honour should have none of these sexual inhibitions that the *never-married girls* have; she should be satisfied with a few tosses of affection here and there, with *small, small* acts of love – she is a mature woman, no? So, no stress! Her maturity is why we like her, her maturity is why we cannot marry her.

Concerns about the age of responsibility (i.e., children's attained age, when single parents may begin to consider a second marriage or dating) are mainly out of consideration for the mental and emotional welfare of the children, given the potential disruptions that the introduction of a third party might cause. In Nigeria, as with many other parts of the world, this is not the primary driver of the negative branding that is targeted primarily at women. It is simply a result of prejudice.

I found this definition on honour-shame cultures that aptly captures the sub-culture I have attempted to describe so far:

> *In honor-shame cultures, you are who you are connected to.*
> *It doesn't matter what you know, but who you know. Life is*
> *about securing a network of connections and relationships.*
> *Children are identified by their parents' name. Two people*
> *who just meet will try to establish some sort of family*

> *connection. Orphans, widows, and barren people endure a lower status because they don't have family around them. Someone without family is a 'nobody'. So, to be a 'somebody', you have to be connected to other people.*[1]

Anne Alexander, 2017

When I look back at the decades since my mother's separation, I see the direct consequence of her shame on me and my siblings. As children, we were within earshot of it – fatherless children, shameless woman – those were the words that people quickly resorted to in the wake of a small argument. So, we carried the shame with her; her silence and shrinking became ours. Every time someone made a negative comment that linked directly or indirectly to my mother's status, my mind penned it away as something not to become, something not to be associated with. I thought surely, she could have made better choices and that I would make sure not to make the same mistakes. It took coming to terms with my convictions, to realise that I had internalised toxic shame at an early age and developed behavioural handicaps that trailed my adulthood.

By my teenage years, I had developed a toxic fear of shame that was the basis for my decision-making. Perfect academic performance and exerting personal standards of decorum became a central rule of my life. The outcome of my negative mental position and perfectionism addiction was that I did not develop coping systems. I had little room to accommodate mistakes in myself and others. To my mind, I was already less than, already handicapped, surely, there was no way that I

---

[1] Anne Alexander, 'A Better Definition of Honor Shaming Cultures – "Connection"', Honor Shame Resources for Global Ministry (15 March 2017) https://honorshame.com/better-definition-honor-shame-cultures-connection/

could accommodate any further criticism. This was the lens through which I also judged the world. My brothers bore the brunt of it. I was constantly shoring them up, asking them to do better, to look better so the world would not think less of us. I recall episodes where I would spiral into a deep depression at the slight criticism, rejection, or failure. My mood swings were epic and so was my isolation. People thought of me as deeply introverted, they had no incline that I was shielding myself, due mostly to my negative mental dialogue. A million words were spoken in my mind daily. Few of them were heard from my lips. A lot of them were unhealthy.

As you would expect, life has completely different sets of rules; the willingness to be perfect is not enough when all the variables are not in your control. It took trauma and conscious practices to realise that I had adopted a perfection-shaming worldview that had become the mirror through which I evaluated life. What was more astonishing was the discovery that in a lot of ways, the rules by which I judged myself and others were not the ones I claimed to uphold. The crucial thing about unidentified personal biases is that they are adopted at such an early age that we don't acknowledge their existence. In my adult years, when asked broadly about my worldview, I spoke often of empathy, tenacity, and growth; not once did I allude to a life coloured by the need to safeguard myself against shame, a need to be perfect at all costs.

Behavioural Shame

Held to a higher standard of morality and respectability, shame is used to enforce female behavioural conformity from early life into their advanced ages. Behavioural shaming for teenage girls manifests in unhealthy stereotypes about their cooking and homemaker capabilities, physical appearance, sexuality, and standards of modesty/feminine respectability. They are less encouraged to participate in physical sports, coerced into stereotypical tasks, yet required to excel academically while maintaining moral piety. Women in their 20s contend with the expected age of marriage attainment, a prevalent perception that their highest attainable status is that of a married woman, and that they must hurry *into settling down* in their 20s, which often translates into missed career kickstart opportunities, and less enthusiasm for pursuits that are critical to their financial and economic security.

Corporate female executives may be pressured to *multitask* - a masked, gendered, disproportionate demand for women to provide homemaking and caregiving responsibilities at the expense of career growth. In reality, coercion to trade-off time spent in professional pursuits contributes to women exiting the world of work. Even within professional settings, women's behaviour is guarded by shame. Exerting standards of behaviour adopted from social norms interplay in professional relationships, placing a disproportionate demand to appear more respectable, more organised, more in charge, yet more feminine; whatever that means. Advanced women are also constrained to behavioural rules that allot to them a certain martyrdom. Matriarchy in Africa seems to connote a lack of interest in self, beauty, sexual expression, and socialisation outside of family groups.

Weaponised shame often leads to debilitating consequences for those on the receiving end. I witnessed first-hand my mother's social shrinking, isolation, and her bending-over-backwards attitude. When I think of her often-conciliatory posture, it brings to mind the image of a woman on her knees, *always on her knees*, in penance, living most of her adult life like a nun in earthly purgatory. It is only in the past decade that I have found the courage to mention the idea of a boyfriend. I would jokingly compliment her and suggest she go out and socialise. I know she has deeply ingrained Christian values, so I would show her pictures or stories I had found online of older, respectable-looking women, who recently got married. The standard response for the past 10 years has been, *I am satisfied with my children; I do not need more.* I am yet to give up on the idea that she might reconsider; maybe someday, she will meet someone. Maybe I will still get to plan the beachfront wedding that I imagine would flatter her. I never got to see her dating; I would very much like to enjoy the amusement of her navigating the drama of romance. It is something I often mention, "Mum, it'll be fun to watch you wear red lipstick like you used to, go out at night, and come back home with that shy girl thing you do once in a while."

While my mum's struggle with shame manifested mainly in waning self-worth, around the world, women's shaming has been associated with self-harm, drug addiction, and behavioural challenges which all result in low life attainment. Social acceptance is a big part of individual identity and personal acceptance. For women, shaming and perfection cultures exact a huge price. When we feel inadequate, our self-dialogue is compromised and if not checked through some sort of validation experience, it leads to habitual negative self-talk that is detrimental to our growth.

Siamese Twins

Across mainstream media, we all share and enjoy imagery that reminds us to be the perfect version of perfect; imagery and language that reinforce stereotypes about the perfect life. The list is endless: the perfect career, beauty, behaviour, parent, age of attainment ... Our identities at any age are influenced by ideals that we learn and internalise. At any age, the media still has the power to influence our subconscious, which informs how we behave. As the media leans on stereotypical ideals and stories in order to gain ground – *following, trending, profit* – it also presents us with versions of reality and truth that inform how we behave, what we behave, and ultimately, what we become.

The ideal story is the basis for which the beauty industry taps into our insecurities and reinforces them until we become addicted to behaviours, inhibitions, and habits that we cannot break. The ideal woman is a figment of imagination that has continued to evolve over time. In Nigeria, I grew up hearing that women with a fuller build were the ideal, that the African woman is a curvy voluptuous woman – full stop. I was often labelled a tomboy for my slender, non-voluptuous features. Conversely, by the time that I got into university, runway model features were the more popular body type and I saw many of the older women in my life labour to become that. My vanity soared during this period with the knowledge that my body type which had previously been *inadequate* was now appreciated. I still had my concerns; I wanted a bigger this and a smaller that, but I would say to myself, "At least I am slender and proportionate." Today, the classic Lagos beauty reference may be a woman who seems to have successfully merged varying body types into one frame. I am not certain she is a classic figure eight. These days, this woman has a ruler slim midsection and a voluptuous bosom and bottom. Her legs are just the right size of thick, not too thick else she looks stocky, not too slender else she looks unbalanced.

I wonder what the next few years hold as we enter the age of filter beauty. Filter beauty is a new beauty rage that has people going under the knife to attain in real life, the replicas of their filtered version. Inspired by digitally augmented versions of self, real and virtual have begun to merge. The long-term outcomes are yet to be fully explored.

Women's objectification (viewing women as sexual objects, relating to women on the merit of their bodies, body parts, and physical features alone, rather than their whole being which combines intellect and other components) is credited with having a significant impact on how women think of themselves and their worth. Objectification leads women to look outward for validation about themselves and their appeal. It causes them to credit or demerit their worth based on the recognition of a third party. Anxiety from objectification and stereotypes is credited with the resort to cosmetic procedures and mental health challenges tied to body image. In a study that evaluates body image opinions across age groups and sexes, Beauty School Directory, an online directory that lists providers of services in the beauty industry, reported that children from ages three to five had already developed strong body image opinions.[2] The report, which shows data from both male and female respondents, captured the ratio of persons with negative body images across demographies and showed a correspondence between body image opinion and:

---

[2] Beauty Schools Directory, 'Body Image: List of Facts, Figures, and Statistics' (2022), https://www.beautyschoolsdirectory.com/blog/body-image-statistics

- Self-rejection: Characterised by negative self-talk, comparing oneself to others, isolation, and a lack of desire to pursue goals; a belief that one is not good enough leading to self-sabotage.
- Body dysphoria: A fixation over one's perceived physical flaw to the point where it begins to affect happiness and quality of life.
- Surgery addiction: Compulsive surgeries to eliminate perceived flaws.

It is more than likely that we will fall short of culture's demand that we consistently look outward to gain validation that is crucial for our self-acceptance. When we fall short, we are subjected to feelings of inadequacy. When that feeling is coloured by groundless dogma, we begin to emulate and aspire to trends and opinions, rather than personal preferences or growth plans that are based on self-acceptance. Inherent in the choice to self-reject is implicit permission to reject others. This rejection of self and others leads to more censure, and a repeated cycle of shaming, more so, in a society where social currency and popularity are increasingly the bedrock of identity.

Perfection fixation breeds abuse and bullying. When we learn to assimilate a singular ideal of something, it closes our minds and makes us less responsive to others. Because the subconscious is the seat of our triggers and responses, we find ourselves towing a line that we do not make a conscious decision to. The *perfect* that we share compulsively and credit with our praises and compliments perpetuates stereotypes that make us insecure and stuck, feeding and reinforcing an often elusive and subjective standard that empowers only a small group of people – those who profit from the commerce of beauty addiction.

The motivation to be the best version of oneself is tied to feelings of acceptance. Innately, our self-acceptance is tied to the esteem that our societies bestow on us individually and collectively. This is why representation and inclusion are crucial in defining moral and behavioural codes. The biblical injunction, to "love your neighbour as you love yourself" implicitly connotes that it is he/she who loves themselves that is then able to love someone else.[3] I believe this carries true anywhere in the world. The task to adopt real representation and design social acceptance around the idea that we must all give pause and lead with empathy is a collective call to action that will see people all over the world break free of social barriers and emerge into a life of attainment.

---

[3] Holy Bible, New International Version, Matthew 22:39

Chapter 2

The Brave & the Desperate

B*ravery* is defined as heroism, putting yourself in a position that is life-threatening or exposing yourself to tough situations. The *Merriam-Webster Dictionary* defines it as "mental or moral strength to face danger."[4] *Desperation* on the other hand is a willingness or desire to achieve something at all costs. It involves taking extreme measures in an attempt to get or escape something.

The *unexpected* is a notion we are all too familiar with – the 40-something-year-old who *finally* finds love, the 50-something who has an affair with someone 20 years younger. Is it desperation for companionship that makes an advanced woman marry a much younger man? Is it desperate to seek romance in one's 60s? Is there underlying bravery in a much-advanced man or woman approaching romance with openness and desire; a belief that they are deserving of

---

[4] Merriam Webster dictionary, https://www.merriam-webster.com/dictionary/brave#h1

passion at whatever age, despite living in a society that communicates that they have expired, that their opportunity to love is done, and they must now retire to predefined *respectable* living?

Our society seems to have simply decided that passion is not for everyone. Young people enjoy romance, young people get married at the *right age*. Because we have determined that companionship and sexual expression are youth-associated because we expect love amongst the elderly to mellow/diminish into a version of familial respect, we are shocked at outliers who simply do not comply with our *normal*, so we make a sensation of them. Our collective shock is not the same for men as it is for women. Around the world, there seems to be a shared acceptance of men's sexuality and romantic participation at almost any age. While men in Nigeria are historically permitted, maybe even encouraged through references to masculine virility, to indulge their sexuality well into their 60s and 70s, for women, that ideal romance/love age diminishes as one inches past 40. When a woman has kids, romance is less associated with her identity. As her children approach marriage age themselves, she is expected to retire into her role as a family matriarch. This is what her identity, respectability, and status are defined by. While a 50-year-old woman without children might be congratulated for *finally* finding love, a mother at the same age might have people wondering why she needs male companionship *in the first place*.

So, where do sexuality and age fit into self-worth? And why is my book title a call to my mother, a grandmother in her 60s, to find love again? It is a question that I am committed to answering in this chapter with experiences, references, and personal stories.

I sat side by side with Mama B, as we fondly called her, over an 18-month period when I held a job with an advertising agency. Mama B was divorced from her first marriage and on the journey to her second. We didn't know this at the time, but when I look back now, I recognise the fortune of that coincidence. She knew of the pressure and rhetoric around my not being married as I approached 30, and I in turn as her work buddy and you might say office confidant shared the humour of her exciting new romance with her then-new boyfriend, now husband. In response to my feeling of being pressured, she told me of the same sense of a clock counting down on her as she approached 30. According to her, she raced into marriage to ensure that she wasn't single at 30. She recalled she had seen the signs of their incompatibility, yet she affirmed her decision to go ahead with her first marriage with a mental note to *se eleyi na* – a common phrase in the Yoruba language, meaning to go ahead with that which is available as a stopgap, even if that option was not entirely palatable, even if the outcomes or future might not be to one's liking.

In 2018, when I started the initial research for this book, my girlfriend, Iretiogo, shared with me the circumstances of her marriage and separation, she spoke of encouragement from religious leaders and her family, to overlook her concerns about the character and status of her intended and go on with a marriage that became a tale of trauma. The notion that love is time-bound for women, or that women may compromise, forgo unanswered questions, their own intuition, in order *to settle down to respectability,* informed a five-year journey through emotional abuse, financial irresponsibility, cheating, and finally abandonment. Despite the obviousness of the situation, Iretiogo would contend with pressure to remain in that marriage, to pray and fast, socially constrained by the idea that it is surely better to endure marriage than to be on the end of the divide – the divorce end that signifies dishonour for both herself and her family.

It has been about a decade since I first tentatively shared my interest in finding my mum a boyfriend/male companion. I recall my growing conviction that her lifestyle was stilted. I knew she could have more from life, the more that neither myself nor my siblings could give to her. The initial scandal and shock from family, friends, and my mum herself embarrassed me. Yet, like a dog with a bone, I did not *leave it alone*. I am happy today that I kept interrogating the idea of my mother finding love, it forced me to question love, to probe her, myself, my society, and our collective beliefs. It helped me to learn about love and its multiple paths, its interplays and boundaries, so much so that I realised that the love my mother needed was not only of the romantic kind, it was the self-kind, a love she needed to give to herself in a way that reaffirmed her to herself, and her place in society. Below, I have attempted to anonymously capture some of the reactions of close friends and family the first time I shared the idea with them.

- M&G: (*an uncomfortable laugh and embarrassed look*) But, why Izin? What are you thinking?
- B: Why? (*aghast expression*).
- O (a male friend who had never met my mum): - Your mum is not interested in that; she is more interested in you finding a husband.
- E: (*laughing*) I don't mind dating her if she will date me.
- S: Show me her picture, let me see if she looks good.
- T: You women are too emotional.
- A: You are such a mummy's girl.

Of the majority that I shared this idea with, only one person in close to 10 years has treated the conversation with some real consideration. He took time to think about my concern, and then simply said, "Yes, marriage will give her a longer life." You may find it some sort of double-edged sword, to know that while I was busy thinking of a million ways to get my mother into some sort of dating pool since I couldn't find a social scene in Lagos that was suitable for her lifestyle (trust me, I looked) she had been equally busy worrying about my age and unmarried status. Yearly, she would tell me stories that likened me to a plant, "Women are like flowers, they wither with time. You should find someone and *settle down*."

My mum definitely plays into the thinking that love and marriage are the preserve of youth. Her continuous reminders about the consequence of late marriage and non-marriage, despite coming from a place of concern, are laced with the belief that there is a time constraint on love, especially as a woman. The question is, to what degree is that concerned with my happiness and growth, rather than a prevailing bias on what my being single *looks like* for us both?

Ageism

Ageism is not a term we are all too familiar with. Most of my respondents what I now call my *find-my-mum-a-boyfriend challenge* in the past decade were likely unaware of an ageist bias. Many responded based on their subconscious beliefs about advanced people, about feminine respectability vis-à-vis romance, love, and marriage. Though references to age discrimination commonly apply to older people, young people face age discrimination too. Life and living seem to have been divided into sections and signals, a herd mentality that passes one along the assembly line based on ideals and prejudice. You get an education at a certain age, then you marry, buy your first car, a house, and on and on. It is common, maybe even generally accepted that we may judge people by age vis-à-vis expectations of attainment at that age.

In addition to attainment markers (signals of success), young people contend with prejudices about the quality of their reasoning. It is not uncommon for younger people to be "shut up" or for their contributions to be discounted simply because they are young.

> *Every second person in the world is believed to hold ageist attitudes – leading to poorer physical and mental health and reduced quality of life for older persons, costing societies billions of dollars each year.*[5]

United Nations, 2021

> *Ageism arises when age is used to categorize and divide people in ways that lead to harm, disadvantage, and injustice. It can take many forms including prejudicial attitudes, discriminatory acts, and institutional policies and practices that perpetuate stereotypical beliefs.*[6]

World Health Organization, 2021

> *The term 'ageism' refers to two concepts: a socially constructed way of thinking about older persons based on negative attitudes and stereotypes about ageing and a tendency to*

---

[5] United Nations, 'Global Report on Ageism' (19 March 2021), https://www.un.org/development/desa/ageing/uncategorized/2021/03/ageist-attitudes-held-by-half-of-the-worlds-population-cause-serious-social-and-economic-ills/
[6] World Health Organization, 'Ageism is a Global Challenge: UN' (18 March 2021), https://www.who.int/news/item/18-03-2021-ageism-is-a-global-challenge-un

> *structure society based on an assumption that everyone is*
> *young, thereby failing to respond appropriately to the real*
> *needs of older persons. Ageism is often a cause for individual*
> *acts of age discrimination and also discrimination that is*
> *more systemic in nature, such as in the design and*
> *implementation of services, programs and facilities. Age*
> *discrimination involves treating persons in an unequal*
> *fashion due to age in a way that is contrary to human rights*
> *law.* [7]

Ontario Human Rights Commission, 2002

In an *Elle* article, titled 'Ageism Hurts All of Us, Even "Young People"', Rainesford Stauffer writes of herself and an older friend's (nearly two decades older) realisation that they both were running out of time. While she felt she was clearly not going to have her life *figured out* by age 25 or 30 or whatever the appropriate age is, her friend grappled with the sensation, spurned by a society that values youth as if it's a moral high ground, that her work had less value the older she got.

"In both directions, our mutual realization highlighted a line of thought embedded in society: that the best parts of our lives, selves, bodies, careers, and identities should be squished into a single decade, the narrow window between age 20 and 30 when we're neither 'too young' to understand or 'too old' to be relevant. This fixation on 'being young'—aka in your twenties—places timestamps on our worthiness

---

[7] Ontario Human Rights Commission, 'Ageism and Age Discrimination (Fact Sheet)' (2002),
https://www.ohrc.on.ca/en/ageism-and-age-discrimination-fact-sheet#:~:text=The%20term%20%22ageism%22%20refers%20to,real%20needs%20of%20older%20persons

that seem to decrease as the number of birthday candles on our cakes increase."[8]

Stauffer wrote about the harmful glorification of youth, including its effect on young people. According to her, "… There are infamous lists of everything we should've done by 30, including so-called markers of adulthood … that always seem to lack acknowledgment of social and economic context in which those decisions might be unfolding. There's a cultural fixation on 'high achievers' who accomplished an extraordinary amount before they made it to the third decade of their lives, making the rest of us wonder how on earth they saved or did that much." She goes on, "We're never without news clips on wunderkinds or a 25-year-old who saved a million dollars, implying not that they're special for having done these things—the so-called impressive part is that they've *done them while they're young*."

Gendered Ageism

Underscoring age discrimination is a sexist belief that the older woman is not sexy and cannot be sexy. Her sexual participation is, therefore, an anomaly that we cannot accommodate. Prejudiced, we simply label people, *women in particular,* as past their prime.

> *Ageism was coined by the famous geriatrician Robert Butler in 1969 to describe 'a distaste for growing old'. It was not until about a quarter of a century later, that the term 'gendered ageism' was introduced and accepted as a way to intersect ageism with sexism. Yet, its pervasive and harmful effect on older women, who form the majority of the older*

---

[8] Rainesford Stauffer, *'Ageism Hurts All of Us, Even "Young People"',* ELLE (6 May 2021), https://www.elle.com/life-love/a36290047/ageism-hurts-all-of-us-even-young-people/

population, has gone largely unrecognised and uncorrected. For example, the greying hair of older men is viewed as distinguished while grey hair in women is considered a negative sign of ageing. With age, men often increase their social status through the accumulation of wealth, while women often feel invisible as they age, being judged on their looks alone..[9]

OECD Forum, 2022

Society's emphasis on what Catalyst defines as 'lookism' which is the importance of a youthful and attractive appearance, puts women under a microscope as they show visible signs of aging. Because of 'lookism', women face ageism earlier than their male counterparts. The bias erodes women's self-esteem and confidence, but the effects of gendered ageism for professional women go beyond the pressure they may feel to look young. This form of bias affects their job security and financial future as they are perceived in the workplace as being less valuable, less competent, and irrelevant as they age..[10]

Bonnie Marcus, 2021

According to research, ageism may now be even more pervasive than sexism. Can you only imagine the devastating consequences it may be for individuals that are subject to the

---

[9] Paula Rochon, Surbhi Kalia, and Paul Higgs, 'Addressing Gendered Ageism: A Better Retirement For All women' The OECD Forum Network (3 March 2022), https://www.oecd-forum.org/posts/addressing-gendered-ageism-a-better-retirement-for-all-women

[10] Bonnie Marcus, *'Gendered Ageism Affects Women's Job Security and Financial Viability'*, *Forbes* (20 September 2021), https://www.forbes.com/sites/bonniemarcus/2021/09/20/gendered-ageism-affects-womens-job-security-and-financial-viability/?sh=63bec0232bc4

> *two? Older women face the accumulated effects of ageism and sexism in several areas of their lives. To start, they are more likely than men to encounter ageist attitudes. They can find themselves facing dual discrimination in access to employment and pensions and to key goods and services in the health and insurance sectors.[11]*

ageingequal.org, 2018

Several women have stories similar to Mama B and Iretiogo's. What begins as a healthy desire for the marriage union can quickly evolve into a do or die pressure, a collective desperation to accomplish matrimony at any cost, at the *right* sounding age, and within a right sounding age difference where the man is expected to be older by a respectable number of years. When such women have the courage to exit an unhealthy marriage thereafter, a fury of interventions, labels and censure are unleashed, often to the degree that they are unable to give romance a second chance.

How many women ever really decide? I mean, how many previously married or single parenting Nigerian/African women decide to explore the dating scene with the intent to find long-term commitment? What proportion of them can consciously socialise, meet partners (single or previously married themselves) in safe and inclusive spaces where their intent to find love, and maybe marriage, is not coloured by exclusions and limitations; where they may date and not stumble through a maze of men who are happy to maintain a sexual connection that is yet limited by a refusal to explore longer-term commitment due to socialised biases? Men, who even if they were inclined to long term commitment, would have to contend with their own mother's opinion,

---

[11] Ageing Equal, 'Ageism and Gender' (2018), https://ageing-equal.org/ageism-and-gender/

what their friends might say, even where *her* children will stay. Children after all belong to their father's houses in Africa. So, how does he raise another man's children?

I recall a conversation between a male friend and me over 10 years ago. What began as exchanging confidences about both our dating lives, evolved into his complaints about his girlfriend's behaviour. He ended his grumble with "I'm dating her despite the fact that she was raised by a single mother." Whatever it was that I felt that day, it must have added to my mutiny and shame over my mother's separation. To this day, I still do not have the words to describe the way I felt at that moment.

Of all the groups that experience ageist biases, single mothers may very well be the worst hit. When we heap a combination of shaming around divorce and/or single parenting status with sexual objectification and age discrimination, we really are piling on a litany. How do we expect that same person to thrive; to maintain a positive picture about themselves and their place in the world? What does that labelling do to their ability to love themselves or someone else? Will they not shrink and shrivel? Will they not try to exit this human form, maybe find an alternative planet, where they may hide from the loss of dignity and acceptance that is seemingly forever out of reach?

Think about it – the right age of attainment, the right age to love, the right way to look, to be deserving of love – such a weight, such a needless weight! Societies that tell us if, to whom, when, and how we can express love contribute to our inability to do the exact thing. The inevitable will happen, women coerced and pressured into marriage will hopefully continue to exit situations that do not benefit them. Sadly, many of such women will contend with a new form of desperation, one that is interwoven in the fabric of our societies – our demand for perfect appearances, for stories that match the narrow frame of our religious and cultural ideals. Desperation before marriage, desperation after marriage, pulling us in these unhealthy directions simply because, and costing us happiness simply because. Ageing is a process that we all must contend with if we are lucky to have a long life in the first place. Unhealthy age stereotypes on the other hand contribute to negative self-talk, self-limiting behaviour, and low quality of life. Taboos and judgement lead people to desperate, rather than brave choices, choices that show that our collective sense of worthiness has been left to the whims of popular culture that is hardly ever found in truth and empathy. Society is no better for it.

> In an attempt to correct norms about social judgement, Colgate-Palmolive (India) Ltd launched a campaign in 2020 titled Begin Again with a Smile. "The story revealed the journey of an elderly woman whose heightened loneliness during the Covid-19 lockdown propelled her to take charge of her life with a decision to find companionship. It describes her experience of overcoming inhibitions and fear of social judgment, leading to a pivotal moment in her life after the lockdown where she embraces a new beginning with optimism and confidently introduces her new partner to her family and loved ones."[12]

This Colgate commercial is the sort of bravery that I allude to in the title of this chapter, and the place from which the title of this book

---

[12] Business Insider, 'Colgate's Endearing Campaign Encourages People to Stop Worrying About "What'll People Think" And Just Follow Their Hearts' (27 August 2020), https://www.businessinsider.in/advertising/brands/article/colgates-endearing-campaign-encourages-people-to-stop-worrying-about-whatll-people-think-and-just-follow-their-hearts/articleshow/77782264.cms

comes. In witnessing my mum's refusal to participate in, or seek romantic companionship, I have wondered, to what degree is her choice informed by a bound identity? Bound by respectability and doctrine? To what degree is she simply exercising her right to choose in all things, as it should be for anyone? Finding love again for some might lead to new beginnings of the romantic kind. For others, it may simply lead to other forms of positive, life-affirming choices. The freedom to do so without prejudice is the lesson.

Chapter 3

Love Tales

I have grappled with romantic love all my life, struggled with my role in it, and the emptiness several romantic relationships have left me with. I struggled with the sense that I was not loved enough, not in the way that I dreamed to be loved. It took a long time to realise that my conflict was dual. First, I had not learned to love myself, to build an ideology about self and love. Secondly, I had failed to define what I needed from companionship. So, in failing to articulate, I had placed a huge, unnecessary burden on love. By failing to understand my needs and what I would give in return, my dating was based on physical attraction and vague assumptions had no clarity, and therefore no reward.

When one fails at romance as a teenager, no one really pays you mind; they don't make much of your not speaking of a boyfriend, your empty valentines' days, or your romance-free birthday celebrations. They likely make nothing of it, after all, you should be busy making your way through academic milestones. You may even get praised for being serious-minded, your parents likely relax a little at the assurance that your virtue and future may not be compromised by risky sexual behaviour.

When that same silence trails your milestone years as an adult, people do notice, and what might initially start as a few inquiries can blow up into a series of interventions, prayers, matchmaking endeavours, and in my case, outright blackmail. When a woman *fails* to get married by 30, it often leads to an outcry. It signals that the worst has happened. Rather than the occasional prodding and pushing, you get a community intervention. Depending on faith and family dynamics, everyone chips in – cousins, aunts, religious leaders, and friends. They get in a race against time to see you *settle down* so you can have a *great life*. Your mentors are called in, on what seems like a pre-planned schedule, you are passed around the family hierarchy in the hope that someone will make sense of you and make sense to you on the urgency and sadness of your predicament.

Underlying the theatrics is a notion that you cannot be happy, in fact, you should not be happy to be single at that age. Your attempts at self-celebration during milestones and victories may be met with indifference from parents who think you have nothing to celebrate. Your married friends might suddenly become sages, suggesting that you spend less time chasing your standards so you can find someone to marry you. Such was the history of my introduction to 30. My mother cried often; the drama, if recorded, would have made for a great movie.

In earlier parts of this book, I shared several accounts of stigmatisation. I wrote about masculine permission and feminine discrimination; I shared about *the transgression* of the single mother and the coercion of the single woman. Here, I will attempt to summarise my understanding of the root causes of the African cultural malaise, the root of shame and pressure that is unfortunately at the heart of the African love story.

Tied to the expectation of feminine virtue in most African cultures, is an insistence, a definition of feminine morality that abides firmly by limited sexual liberty, the demand for self-denial, and an insistence on chastity, demureness, and pretence if necessary, all aimed at *an ideal identity, a brand* that culminates in the married woman status. This lack of agency and self-acknowledgement make it almost taboo for the African woman to accept, address, or cultivate her sexual desires outside the boundaries of a marriage union.

Built on this insistence, is an ideology of love and loving with such a narrow perspective that love outside the marriage union, between husband and wife, is perceived, at best regarded as a much younger, much inferior sibling. The single woman of marriageable age really has only one choice, to find someone to marry her, because *superior love, real love, is really only available in that union.*

Then of course the communal impact of that demand, the collective identity that the woman who does not make a quick marriage paints her inner circle with, she is not only the lady whose peers married ahead of, she is the lady by whom her mother, aunty, and siblings are defined. In casual conversation, she stains her collective by being the one anomaly. This ideology is firmly entrenched in Africa, and indeed, in many parts of the world. It is a driving force behind the feminine pressure of marriage attainment at all costs. In a sense, in the culture that I describe, you do not love just for yourself, your sexuality is not yours alone, you do not marry just for yourself; your attainments are a collective, and your pressure to attain proof of your adulthood is as essential to you as it is to your social circle.

Inherent in culture is a myth that we should be similar to be a collective. Unfortunately, the idea that we must all be the same, garbed in the same status and stature to be communal is the foundation of discrimination and social injustices across the world. The inability to accommodate otherness, our punishment of otherness, is in fact non-inclusive. We cannot love fully if we are stuck on the look and feel of it, on how it fits with us and how it fits with them. It causes us to go about life in judgement. What many African communities have is a collective ideology, meaning satisfaction and esteem from our family connections, stemming from the intent and commitment to the good of all rather than oneself alone. What we clearly miss is the inclusiveness condition.

Where Romance Fails

I do not believe that any one person can love us completely; I do not believe that one person's love is all that we need. As our lives are social, so our loving is. I believe that love needs multiple expressions and therefore, multiple conduits back to us. When we presume that romantic love is the only variation we need, we may soon despair in its insufficiency; we may find that our lives feel empty even in the embrace of a romantic companion – someone whom we love and believe loves us in return. We should picture love for what it is, as a whole bucket, a treasure trove of connections and connecting that makes life richer, a circle of influence that carries us to happiness, even in moments when we forget how to get there.

Romance is not enough and cannot be enough. It is not enough as a basis for growth, it is not enough as a foundation for a lasting marriage, nor as a basis for life attainment. Romance is built on attraction, and attraction only deepens into a rewarding act of love when the parties involved can navigate their relationship with a firm commitment to choices and actions that add value and enhance each other. In cases when this does not happen, romance soon fades off and with it the will to love. It is easy to think of romance as love's high point, life's high point, and yes, for many, it is the peak of intense emotional experience. Yet, we must be wary of exalting that emotional intensity, without consideration for the other crucial aspects of loving. Where romance may be the beginning, love is the process and the end. It is essential to allow ourselves an expansive perspective of love, not only with a romantic companion but also with a range of loving relationships, with a clear knowledge and respect for where each of them fits. It is crucial to develop a deep appreciation and value for our multiple *lovers,* the people, and the experiences that we are *in love with*.

I have made the mistake in time past of taking my lovers for granted, taking leave of my senses at the beckoning of romantic love. I had no real understanding of what love meant; I assumed that romantic love, was, had to be, all that loving encompassed. In my experience, women will ignore, misuse, and undervalue the opportunity to be loved by themselves, family, mentors, and friends, as they remain fixated on an ideal, a love they have decided is the ultimate. In some cases, loving relationships are abandoned at the demand of commitment to a life partner. I have seen instances where women were advised to cut ties to their past before marriage, in order not to allow those ties to rock the new life they had begun. A cousin was advised to change her mobile phone number right before her marriage ceremonies commenced.

The necessity of selection, of evaluating one's life before marriage, and determining what and whom one takes along is a human right. The invalidation of that right to choose is an abuse of it. This gendered necessity of erasure is tied to the burden of *virtuousness* which I mentioned earlier. Not often have I heard this dogma being communicated to men. They seem to have an unspoken grace to keep a range of relationships that validates and affirms them through love practices that are crucial for one's overall well-being.

In recent times, there have been debates and calls for a different approach to storytelling and movies targeting young girls. The demand for fairytales that show young girls being the hero in their own stories hinges on the belief that movies where women are allocated dependent roles that convey them as weak and dependent, prepare them for a life of neediness and low self-efficacy, without a belief in personal acumen and capabilities; I couldn't agree more.

Like the rescued princesses of our fairytales, we women wait for our prince so that our life can begin. Sustaining this behaviour are patriarchal role stereotypes and symbolisms that tell the girl child that she is a transient visitor in her parent's home, that her real place is not with her immediate family. Her name, her inheritance, and therefore her individuality, are in her husband's house and until she gets there, she is simply passing through. So, she anticipates her arrival at her *destination* – her identity, in essence. She invalidates the many loves and opportunities to love that pave her way through life, she doesn't see them, she just doesn't. She loses sight of the multiplicity of life and the chance to live many legacies in one lifetime through a collective of love and lovers. When this anticipation is not met, she shrinks, she shrivels at the unkindness of her label, the one that she joins others in calling herself. She submits to persuasions and practices that further harm her already stressed esteem. Her cover of sadness, her disgrace to the family keeps her perpetually stagnant. How, and where does she go from there? How does she begin to redefine attainment and purpose?

And for the woman who earned this high honour, how does she give it up? Who will she and us both become without her *brand*? the signal of ownership that cements her place in society? To be owned is surely far better; her unhappiness is surely not as important, she must make do so we can all be happy, so there are no oddities, no ambiguities, no embarrassments, so our herd can continue to look good even in cases where we know we are not good. Both she and us, knowing, yet, unwilling and fearful to change her situation – *unbrave*.

As with all sensationalism, love packaged singly as passion, and sold as a limited-edition ideal between two people is a best-selling movie. Romantic love may be the pinnacle of intense emotional experiences for many, yet, pinnacles need valleys, they need something to stand on when they face the storms of life. A narrow perspective of love often leads to no valleys and no support system. When the storms come, and they will, a deeper perspective of love, a range of love anchors, and lovers are the things that keep us wholesome.

Why Defining Love to Self is Essential

Collective norms are not always in our best interest. Pop culture is not always in our best interest. Ambiguity about love, which is often the basis for crucial life decisions, often leads to regret. These are some of the reasons we must define love. By defining it, we guard our own life choices and can put our foot firmly on the ground rather than carry forward legacies that we do not understand.

Defining love is different from self-love. Self-love encompasses a range of actions and affirmations of oneself that are built on the acceptance of one's flaws, strengths, and weaknesses – all-inclusive. It is what we do to nurture ourselves emotionally and mentally and to affirm our place. I do share more on this later in this chapter. A personal definition of love, on the other hand, is concerned with having a perspective on what love means. It is about finding the right words to answer what love means to us. Definitions enable us to appreciate love when we see it and to recognise when it is absent. When we have no clear understanding of what love means, we pander to dogma and misinformation. Our love acts are guided by stereotypes and worse still, we find it challenging to articulate what we need from our partners and relationships.

Things that we do not understand do not often bring us real value and meaning that our soul connects with. When our connection to love is vague, we go through the motions to the degree that we know, then we flounder and pander, and are unable to do our part to keep our love relationships on track or to at least evaluate them for their merit. Sometimes, we get lucky; in that confusion, we find someone who walks the path with us, and we both emerge with clarity. While social references to love may be a good place to start our exploration, they are not enough to bring us to a place of real conviction and clarity on how to love and receive the love that matches our unique context and personalities.

So, What is Love?

> *Where the myth fails, human love begins. Then we love a human being, not our dream, but a human being with flaws.*[13]

Anaïs Nin, c.1966

> *People think a soul mate is your perfect fit, and that's what everyone wants. But a true soul mate is a mirror, the person who shows you everything that is holding you back, the person who brings you to your own attention so you can change your life.*[14]

Elizabeth Gilbert, c.2006

> *Love never dies a natural death. It dies because we don't know how to replenish its source. It dies of blindness and errors and betrayals. It dies of illness and wounds; it dies of weariness, of witherings, of tarnishings.*[15]

Anaïs Nin, c.1966

In Bell Hooks' *All About Love*, she echoes definitions of love that are held both by herself and some of the greatest writers on the subject, who anchor love on choice rather than instinct.[16] These definitions are the ones that I adopt and consider crucial for a wholesome love experience. They include:

---

[13] https://www.goodreads.com/quotes/761854-where-the-myth-fails-human-love-begins-then-we-love
[14] Kidadl, 'Elizabeth Gilbert's Quotes From "Eat Pray Love"' (2022), https://kidadl.com/articles/best-eat-pray-love-quotes-by-elizabeth-gilbert
[15] https://www.goodreads.com/quotes/777-love-never-dies-a-natural-death-it-dies-because-we
[16] Bell Hooks, *All About Love*, (New York: William Morrow Paperback, 2001)

> *Love is the will to extend one's self for the purpose of nurturing one's own or another's spiritual growth.*[17]

M. Scott Peck, 1979

> *Love is the active concern for the life and the growth of that which we love. Where this active concern is lacking, there is no love.*[18]

Erich Fromm, 1956

> *… Love is as love does. Love is an act of will—namely, both an intention and an action. Will also implies choice. We do not have to love. We choose to love.*[19]

M. Scott Peck, 1979

> *Love is a skill rather than an enthusiasm.*[20]

Alain de Botton, 2017

---

[17] M Scott Peck, culled from *All About Love*
M Scott Peck, *The Road Less Traveled: A New Psychology of Love, Traditional Values and Spiritual Growth* (New York: Simon & Schuster, 1979)
Quote also available at https://www.goodreads.com/quotes/150190-love-is-the-will-to-extend-one-s-self-for-the
[18] Erich Fromm, culled from *All About Love*.
Erich Fromm, *The Art of Loving*, (New York: Harper Perennial Modern Classics, 2019, (first published 1956))
Quote also available at https://www.goodreads.com/quotes/3244826-love-is-the-active-concern-for-the-life-and-the
[19] M Scott Peck, culled from *All About Love*.
M Scott Peck, *The Road Less Traveled: A New Psychology of Love, Traditional Values and Spiritual Growth* (New York: Simon & Schuster, 1979)
Quote also available at https://www.goodreads.com/quotes/150190-love-is-the-will-to-extend-one-s-self-for-the
[20] Alain de Botton culled from *All About Love*
Alain de Botton, *The Course of Love*, (New York: Simon & Schuster, 2017)
Quote also available at https://www.goodreads.com/quotes/7656760-love-is-a-skill-not-just-an-enthusiasm

In All About Love, which I recommend in a list below alongside other books published by the above-mentioned authors, Hooks ties in the ability to love others to self-love. Loving others is in essence a function of what we know to do for ourselves in answer to the need for love. The actions and choices we take daily to ensure that we provide love to ourselves are the same actions that we need to be loving to others. This was a real revelation for me. Firstly, it answered my nagging questions and feelings about being unloved. Secondly, it also defines love in a way that opens it up and makes it relatable. While it might be hard to determine exactly what it means to love someone else, we do know how being loved makes us feel, and that in itself gives us an entry into the acts, commitments, and practices that we need to love ourselves. These same acts and practices are then what we can give to others in the form of love for them. This paradigm is essential in the world that we live in today. Just knowing that love starts with self-love simplifies the concept and makes it more attainable. It gives us a way to find our place in it.

Will means choice and action. These are two words that are central to the four definitions of love that I've highlighted and adopted. They imply that love is not passive. Love builds because of day-to-day choices, backed by day-to day-actions. Oddly, that is not the popular projection of passionate love. Love is pitched as an emotional high that *happens* to us. That emotional high is an intense attraction, there is no denying its existence, yet that attraction is not love.

Does the majority of humanity know and understand this fully? I am not so sure; it is definitely a revelation to me. I had previously put too much stock in the power of my attraction to someone who was not necessarily making choices or taking actions that held benefits for me.

We can hope to find people who have a decent set of values, similar perspectives, and preferences; we can hope that they decide to be concerned with choices and actions that benefit us; we can tell when choices and actions over time hold no value for us, and we can decide what to do with that knowledge. The mutual choices and actions that underscore attraction are the holy grail of succeeding in love.

Both Peck and Fromm emphasise a commitment to growth in their definitions. Commitment to one's growth – a reflection of healthy self-love, commitment to a companion's growth – is an indicator of healthy love for someone else, a partner, friend, a romantic lover.

Leading with Self-Love

Self-love is at the heart of emotional well-being which in turn creates an affirming internal environment for personal growth and intelligence to thrive. It would be great to simply be born with the right amount of love to navigate life's complexities with little impact, but that is not the way life is designed. Self-love is grown and nurtured, it is not simply gifted. Failing to attain social marks of attainment and our own success plans, may incite disappointment, loss of one's sense of purpose and willpower, and negative self-dialogue. Self-nurturing practices which I describe further using the illustration below are part of a continuous personal growth practice that I build upon in the following chapters.

Figure 3.1 **Relationship between self-love and self-efficacy, self-esteem & self-concept**

Through self-loving, which combines the practice of affirmation, empathy, actions, and vulnerability, we can get rid of biases, make real assessments, and change where we need to. Actions of self-love make us less wary about life, less obsessed with competition and comparison and more enabling of ourselves and others. It teaches us that it is okay to have a blueprint that didn't quite play out as planned. It is okay to realise that one's blueprint was designed on the wrong premise and that one needs a new vision of life.

1. Awareness: Loving oneself begins with knowing oneself. Much more than anything else, a huge part of self-loving is developing the ability to spend time with oneself, listening, hearing, identifying one's desires, evaluating what one comes from, and why one might be a certain way. This time with self is where we build articulation, we can then tell our brains and our behaviour that this is what I need from me, this is what I need from others. That unambiguity is the catalyst for other acts of self-love. It is how we go from engaging in life based on predetermined markers of our identity to ownership and firm choices on what fulfils our uniqueness.

2. Acts: Acts of self-care can range from mundane to extraordinary: retail therapy, holidays, gifts to oneself, self-affirming words, an educational investment, gratitude, connecting with others, etc. Acts of self-care are an opportunity to enhance our lives with experiences that we have always aspired to.

3. Empathy: Empathy to self and others is a self-love act all in one. Being able to affirm one's flaws, tendencies, and strengths is an act of self-love. Doing that for others, by emotionally connecting with them is another act of self-love. By learning to empathise with ourselves, we can *hold our own hands* when we hurt or fall short of our expectations.

Empathy and love are related, and there is a reason. Empathy as an affirmation practice builds the inspiration to be the best version of self. When we feel empathised with, we are more likely to be motivated rather than overwhelmed by a sense of inadequacy or mistakes. We all thrive and are inspired by empathy. Many of the world's success stories carry an account of empathy, stories of pivotal moments when someone accepted, acknowledged, sacrificed, or gave a hand.

Empathy is not the same as accommodating the demands of an interdependent collective simply because *that is what we do*. No, as we grow, individuals must separate and journey by themselves. Inherent in that individualism is empathy to self that is crucial to what we then bring back to our collective in the form of love and kindness.

4. Vulnerability: The practice of vulnerability is one that enhances our opportunity to live a life of attainment. Insecurity breeds a need to hide and posture, vulnerability allows one to grow and connect. Inner cycle confidants in the form of friends, role models,

mentors, and peer mentors are a great way to have a healthy system of vulnerability, accountability, and support. In close proximity, and if we allow them, they become mirrors that show when we may be blindsided or tunnelled-visioned. They help us to grow into the versions of ourselves that we can truly respect and love, versions that inspire us to remain happy. Through vulnerability to self, we can acknowledge our own needs and spend time building up where we should build up, and reducing what should be reduced.

Self-love and narcissism are completely different. "Self-love is an honest and authentic appreciation for the self, while narcissism is all about proving that you're better than everyone else and making sure others see you as you want to be seen. Self-love is self-focused, while narcissism is other-focused."[21]

Self-Efficacy

Self-efficacy is a person's belief in their ability to succeed in a particular situation.[22] "A strong sense of efficacy enhances human accomplishment and personal well-being. People with high assurance in their capabilities approach difficult tasks as challenges to be mastered rather than as threats to be avoided."[23] A strong self-efficacy is

[21] Cortney E Ackerman, 'What is Self-Compassion and What is Self-Love?' Positive Psychology (2022) https://positivepsychology.com/self-compassion-self-love/

[22] Kendra Cherry, Self Efficacy and Why Believing in Yourself Matters (2020), https://www.verywellmind.com/what-is-self-efficacy-2795954

[23] Albert Bandura, "Self-efficacy" in V. S. Ramachaudran (Ed.), *Encyclopedia of Human Behavior* (Vol. 4, pp. 71-81). New York: Academic Press, (reprinted in H. Friedman [Ed.]), *Encyclopedia of Mental Health*, (San Diego: Academic Press, 1998). Also available at

displayed in how people respond to tough situations, how much gravitas they bring to failure, and how they approach life's obstacles. One's ability to recover from setbacks, push oneself to acquire new knowledge, and navigate new challenges is tied to self-efficacy. Weak self-efficacy on the other hand connotes a tendency to give up on things too quickly, focus on failures, and internalise the outcomes of one's mistakes, rather than using it as a learning opportunity. It is low self-belief.

Self-Esteem

To esteem something is to place value on it. If we think of something as worthy and valuable, we respond to it differently than when we think it isn't. Intricately linked to self-concept, esteem levels determine our ability to either rise to the occasion when confronted by life.

Self-Concept

This is both inside-out and outside-in. By this, I mean that self-concept isn't something we may define by simply standing on the sidelines of life and randomly determining whom we think we might be. Real self-concept is arrived at as we navigate life and identify with our values and preferences in relation to the world. Self-concept is at the root of our motivations, our goals, and what we want to be associated with. I call it both inside-out and outside-in because we navigate self-concept daily. Confronted with new ideas and ideologies, we evaluate them and decide if they fit. We weigh truth, un-thruth, merit, value, and decide what stays and what doesn't. As we live and socialise, we meet with

https://www.uky.edu/~eushe2/Bandura/BanEncy.html#:~:text=People%20with%20high%2 0assurance%20in,maintain%20strong%20commitment%20to%20them.

something that reminds us of ourselves, something we may never have encountered before, yet, we recognise it, we collect it, we shake its hands and we say, "Welcome home" – *inside-in*.

At the same time, self-concept is an outside-in concept. As children, we are born without an incline who we are. We rely on others to guide us to an ideology and that becomes our identity until our teenage years when personal reasoning accelerates, and we explore life based on our deductions. Even when we have reached maturity, the journey of self-concept continues to unfold. We confront signals, definitions, and expectations of who we should be that is based on culture and society – *outside-in*". What we make of those expectations becomes part of our identity. In essence, self-concept is one's personal identity - what we think of ourselves.

Further Reading

1. Bella Hooks, *All About Love* (New York: William Morrow Paperback, 2001) https://www.amazon.com/All-About-Love-New-Visions/dp/0060959479

2. Erich Fromm, *The Art of Loving* (New York: Harper Perennial Modern Classics, 2019) https://www.amazon.com/Art-Loving-Erich-Fromm/dp/0061129739

3. Alain De Botton, *The Course of Love* (New York: Simon & Schuster, 2017) https://www.amazon.com/Course-Love-Novel-Alain-Botton/dp/1501134515/ref=sr_1_1?crid=TUO8S4T70R9&keywords=Alain+De+Botton+%E2%80%93+The+Course+of+Love&qid=1646190016&s=books&sprefix=alain+de+botton+the+course+of+love%2Cstripbooks%2C81&sr=1-1

Chapter 4

Who Am I?

Identity is dependent on the journey we take through childhood into adulthood. Our early exposures determine our subconscious values and beliefs about life. At this point in our lives, we usually adopt an identity that is based on what we see others defined by. It is in adulthood that we begin the necessary journey of questioning and validating the truths and misinformation we internalised in our formative years. Yet, in adulthood, we will continue to encounter many untruths. The assumption, however, is that we have sufficiently developed the capability to validate truth and lie accurately. It is assumed that to a degree we have made claims to the perspectives that matter to us, taken personal journeys, and built self-sufficiencies and codes for life. That is often not the case. In many ways, we may grow and attain key milestones, yet the very nature of life's design can keep us towing preset paths, goals, and ideologies with little consideration for what they mean or matter to us. As Anais Nin puts it:

> *We do not grow absolutely, chronologically. We grow sometimes in one dimension, and not in another; unevenly. We grow partially. We are relative. We are mature in one realm, childish in another. The past, present, and future mingle and pull us backward, forward, or fix us in the present. We are made up of layers, cells, constellations.*[24]

Anais Nin, c.1966

In an article titled 'What It Means to Have a Trauma of Identity', Marta Thorsheim, therapist and founder of the Institute for Traumawork in Norway, defines a healthy identity as:

> *... the sum of all our conscious and unconscious life experiences. Including our beautiful days and our traumatizing ones. We are not denying any part of ourselves... we are integrated with our senses, our feelings, our thoughts, our memories, our will, and our behaviors. It also means that we don't lose ourselves in relationships with others. We are not sacrificing any part of our identity to anyone else.*[25]

Marta Thorsheim, 2022

According to her:

> *When we're children, so many of our early experiences are formative. In extreme situations—and even not so extreme, because as small children, we are very vulnerable—we often have to give up parts of our identity to survive. Whether it's violence, or rejection from a bonding person at a very early*

---

[24] https://www.goodreads.com/quotes/64155-we-do-not-grow-absolutely-chronologically-we-grow-sometimes-in

[25] Marta Thorsheim, 'What It Means to Have a Trauma of Identity', Goop (2002), https://goop.com/wellness/health/what-it-means-to-have-a-trauma-of-identity/

> *stage of development, we start to give up parts of our identity to endure. That can lead us to a trauma of identity. We start to overidentify with others, and in a way our identity can become enmeshed with the identity of, say, our mother. We end up in a state of survival identity and not in a place where we really know who we are.*[26]

Marta Thorsheim, 2022

In the previous chapter, I wrote about my failure at romance, which linked to my failure to love myself. I also wrote about how I had internalised my mother's shame, in response to negative slurs to the degree that I began to protect myself by telling versions of the truth that made us both look good. I was internalising my mother's identity without knowing it. My response to shame and shameful situations directly emulated a shrinking, hiding behaviour. I took offence, yet had no outlet for that offence. Like my mother, I stewed in the shame quietly, internalised it, and became strongly averse and sensitive to any sort of embarrassment. My personality was *easily shamed*.

Wholesome identities are not built on half-truths. Half-truths allude to something we need to hide. Early sexual encounters left me with this need to hide. Coerced into sex much earlier than I wanted, molested severally, and suddenly without my virginity (a crucial part of my identity as a teenage girl raised under strict Christian doctrine), caused me to resent sex. I resented anyone who asked it of me. I wanted to be left alone, yet I wanted to be loved, to have a boyfriend like the rest of my friends, to be carefree, and to live the reality of my romantic fantasies. My handicap and conviction all at once were that I did not want romance earmarked by sex. My second handicap was that I never

---

[26] Marta Thorsheim, 2002

spoke about the abuse. At some point, I gave up on the notion of young romance, I subconsciously decided that if love was tied to sex, then I didn't want it. Being continuously pursued by men young and old, who would often ask about my virginity at my refusal to consummate, and whose *but you are not a virgin* response to my refusal was like a whip to my back, built a complete distaste for the idea. Not once encountering someone willing to love me without the pre-condition of sex made my resolve absolute. This conflicted identity, the struggle with my place in the light of my family's social standing was the identity that I took into adulthood.

We can appear to be growing rapidly in some life directions yet be completely stuck in other areas. That was my life in early adulthood. Rape stilted my maturity, coloured my self-esteem, and muted my growth. I was no longer a good girl and being a good girl mattered to me; it was my *brand*, who I was as a child to my parent and as a Christian. Constantly dogged by Christian doctrine on pre-marital sex combined with the commonplace cultural repression of my sexuality, scarred by sexual brutality, I had no tolerance for anyone's sexual gratification at my expense, to the degree that I questioned my sexuality. I took no joy in sex, yet, I had a growing appetite for it.

I lived in fear that I would end up like my mother; it was death to me, the same way it would be death to her. We were both stuck in this dogma about life; we were both, working the dance of ensuring that I came out with a different story – a better story so that I would fit in places where she hadn't. I become a perfection junkie. My intense scrutiny was both of myself and others. I was hell-bent on perfection because perfection meant unbroken, it meant honour and winning, a balm to my rather insecure personality. I chased it with all that I had.

What chasing perfection did not prepare me for was the necessary journey of failure; for the wherewithal to rise above guilt, mistakes, and foolishness as a necessary step to success at anything in life; and to give myself another chance, as many chances as it was necessary, even when I did not perform to my standards. So, I ultimately failed at failure in my adulthood, the same way I failed at love as a teenager.

When we live based on misinformation and half-truths, we soon fall prey to foolishness, to the demands our minds and society place on us to uphold that which need not be upheld, and to chase acquisition that had no real meaning to us in the first place. Much more than that, we give up the ability to make a sound judgement on our experiences. In many instances, I have arrived at places that I had no intention to journey to, dated people that I knew subconsciously not to date, and denied myself journeys that I should have taken long before I got the courage to. It has taken me much longer than I would have liked to begin to like and recognise myself. As Chinua Achebe puts it:

> *Nobody can teach me who I am, you can describe parts of me, but who I am – and what I need – is something I have to find out myself.*[27]

Chinua Achebe, c.1960

Sometime in 2016, I simply realised that I did not know who I was nor whom I wanted to be. I was making a decent career, some of my goals up to that point had been actualised, yet I felt unfulfilled. The prevailing thought on my mind was that *I am not on my stage*. It felt odd to think of life as a stage. It felt scary and self-absorbed to be much

---

[27] The Famous People, '70 Powerful Chinua Achebe Quotes', (2002), https://quotes.thefamouspeople.com/chinua-achebe-1044.php

more interested in finding my stage than anything else. Earlier, I wrote about making a conscious claim on our identity in diverse ways. Some through birth circumstances, and early life practices, will navigate day-to-day milestones and arrive at clear personal convictions. For others, trauma, new discoveries, or life threats, force a personality conflict that must be resolved. In my case, a crisis of multiple traumas was occurring without my knowledge of it, unhappiness was bubbling to the surface, driven by repressed memories, unattended pain, and the continued pressure to attain people's expectations of me.

Imagine a fit teenager whose manner reminds you of an advanced woman in her 70s, whose steps are tentative, with less and less enthusiasm for socialising. It is a difficult thing to imagine. Yet, this is exactly how I thought of myself several years leading to 2016 – exhausted, dragging along, sleepy. In reality, I slept through most of my leisure time. I shuttled between despair and anger, resentment, and discouragement, and it reflected in my temperament. Anger was an easy outlet and I blamed others when my behaviour was uncivil.

I had no identity, if I did, I could not articulate it to myself. I lived by and for what others wanted and what others had because it looked good. It made them look good and I did not know how to look good to the person who mattered the most, myself. My self-dialogue was filled with what I might have had, what I didn't have, and what it seemed like I would never have. No identity, no story, no inspiration. *When we give less to self, we give less to others.*

Social Versus Personal Identity

Malcolm Gladwell's opening chapter in his best-selling book *Outliers* remains one of the pivotal reads of my life. It signalled the beginning of my rebirth and I have reexamined many of its principles over and over again. In the opening chapter of the book, he writes about the stereotypical stories of success that sell the idea that people succeed purely on the merit of their hard work and personal exception. He references stories of biographies and self-acclaimed successes that are often an inaccurate depiction of what it takes to be successful in holistic terms – stories that do not capture the role of culture, acquired rules of behaviour, and socialisation on one's success trajectory.

He quips:

> *I want to convince you that personal explanations of success don't work. People don't rise from nothing. We do owe something to parentage and patronage. The people who stand before kings may look like they did it all by themselves. But in fact, they are invariably the beneficiaries of hidden advantages and extraordinary opportunities and cultural legacies that allow them to learn and work hard and make sense of the world in ways others cannot. It makes a difference where and when we grew up. The culture we belong to and the legacies passed down by our forebears shape the patterns of our achievement in ways we cannot begin to imagine. It's not enough to ask what successful people are like, in other words. It is only by asking where they are from that we can unravel the logic behind who succeeds and who doesn't.[28]*

Malcolm Gladwell, 2008

This opening from *Outliers* literally changed my life. It caused me to rethink a lot of the nuances that I took for granted, it had me ask the question, where are you from? I realised that I would not succeed or go

---

[28] Malcolm Gladwell, *Outliers: The Story of Success,* (New York: Hachette Audio, 2008)

as far as I dreamed if I continued to hunch my back based on limitations and biases. I learned through *Outliers*, the value of *entitlement* as a cultural advantage – a group of learned behaviours (negotiation, dialogue with elders, power dynamics, socialising) that enables young children to build a confident, independent identity earlier in life. I learned to seek the unspoken and accept answers only after I had fully understood what they meant.

To understand self and be useful for self, we must understand where we are from and exactly what that means for the life we have lived and the life we may make in the future. The culture that we are born into underlies the way that we engage in living and ultimately success. In the earlier chapters, I shared stories about marriages endured to fulfil expectations and avoid taboos, women cultivated for a future that fits the frame of social preferences, ageist barriers that limit power and self-efficacy in young people and advanced persons alike. When we are left with defining self by society, we suffer at its behest. What it says becomes our law and order. We are in a sense already bound, yet free. Before the answer to the question of who we are, we then must answer the question, Where am I from?

Gladwell's insight can be summarized as *people succeed based on who they are, and who they are is determined by what and where they come from*. To further extend this phrase, one might say that *attainment is determined by identity*. One might then suggest that an ambiguous, limiting identity may derail one's life attainment and vice versa.

Our task is to untangle early and to keep untangling so we can live a life of meaning. It is not enough to broadly understand that one should have a clear personal identity, it is important that we define it, and that we take defining it as a continuous concern, as relevant to life as eating and drinking. By doing so, we enhance the quality of our lives and we also add value to society as we model a new way of thinking in a world that is hardly designed to change its *definition of purpose, or identity* if no one pushes for it. In a world where people are easily branded even before they have a chance to discover themselves, my dream is to see more women rise to self-actualisation with personal clarity and motivation, rather than with self-deprecating and trepidation.

Ageing Backwards

So how does one untangle from a life defined by others into a life cultivated for one's fulfilment? My simple response is *Age Backwards.*

The ageing backwards approach is a model of lifelong learning that I first coined in 2017 as I made my way through a series of life-transforming practices. This season marked my reawakening; it signalled questioning and accelerated growth, and I have come to describe it as my *coming to life.* Five years ago, when I wrote about ageing backwards, I thought of it as a series of wellness products that would lead to a wellness practice. Today, I think of it as a life practice that may incorporate products at the users' will.

Ageing Backwards

To stumble, like a child
To lean forward as sage
To be the alfa and omega
To yet be the babe at suckle
To be the first, yet be the last
Willingly, channelling
Through galaxies and oceans
Becoming as it was

Becoming as intended
A million lifetimes in one
Advancing, without resistance.

We think of ageing as a physical phenomenon, as a timeline of life as we count the years. In ageing backwards, I propose a mindset that simply says, "I will age backwards." To age backwards, we are compelled to adopt the mental stance of a lifelong learner. To be less inclined to stick with what we already know, the life we have already planned or succeeded at, and become inclined to explore that which we do not know with vulnerability and curiosity. To advance into youth and buoyance as we grow older rather than limit ourselves to the idea that we know or should know the right thing simply because we are adults. To suddenly realise that each of us has the opportunity to live multiple lifetimes in one lifetime and that one's past or present does not matter as much as the future. To age backwards is to advance without resistance.

Nature tends to protect our self-image. As we advance, we build habits, desires and rituals, we make claims to knowledge and wisdom. - These become our assuredness. With that assuredness comes our resistance and undoing. We now know, we do not need to know more, we have arrived at finite. We stop growing. The truth I have found is that several convictions and milestones are adopted from a narrow perspective, and many of our dreams likewise. Knowing this, our only choice is really to be willing to reconceive our plans, re-affirm who we are, redefine attainment, in essence, have our identities grow through life with us.

Combined with the life tools which I share in the concluding chapters, the ageing backwards mindset embraces values like vulnerability, growth mindset, and inspiration which I explain below.

Vulnerability Again

Silence is a power tool. Instinctively, we use it to cover inadequacy. Curling up like babies, we excuse handicaps for wisdom and preference. The famous biblical saying "even fools are thought wise if they keep silent, and discerning if they hold their tongues" and its commonly used variety, credited to Abraham Lincoln, "better to remain silent and be thought a fool than to speak and to remove all doubt" is not to be confused with mental voices that tell us to keep quiet when we should speak up.[29] The opportunity to speak up is not the exclusive of the wise or the all-knowing, speaking up is a tool that even the *foolish* must use for clarity, opportunities, inclusion, healing, questioning, and growth. The fleeting benefit of silence is that people may not see our inadequacies, but the bigger consequence is that we also do not see our inadequacies. Vulnerability is not only about us in relation to others, but also about us in relation to us, acknowledging one's strengths and weaknesses, and outlining them unambiguously.

Speaking and learning without the presumption of one's knowledge is wisdom itself. Clarity and vulnerability reside side by side. To question in a sense is to be vulnerable. To say: this doesn't add up, this response or that message doesn't connect, or I don't have the answers that I am supposed to have at this point in my life. Rather than faking it, we can

---

[29] Holy Bible, New International Version, Proverbs 17:28

open up to the opportunities all around us to learn and become the version of ourselves we develop a deep appreciation for.

Vulnerability precedes self-acceptance and enables us to confront our insecurities positively. It helps us to evolve from silent resentments and pride-laced concealment. In vulnerability we embrace our quirks, the things that others find odd and peculiar, the things that we were so stumped on, so bent on hiding. When we expose our insecurities, we are finally able to laugh at them. Where we once obsessed about being mocked, we permit laughter, even encourage it because we are also laughing at this thing about us that we recognise as funny, quirky, or unique.

In embracing vulnerability, I gave up the necessity of erasure; suppressed memories no longer had the power to cause pain and conflict. They became part of my story; one I was comfortable telling. Only after, did I begin to build the resilience that I needed to process life and find healing. I knew my tendencies, I understood exactly why I acted the way that I did. I arrested my negativity, I told it, "No, not today." The moment you know your version of foolishness, the moment you know that your anger or weaknesses will rise at a certain trigger, or that you compulsively act in the same way in certain situations, that is the moment when identity takes over. From there on, seemingly impossible to break habits stand a chance at real reformation.

Practical vulnerability starts with taking note of the things you feel confident about, and the things you feel insecure about. Spend some time thinking about how you responded to those insecurities in the past and finally, outline a new response for the future. Keep this list in a journal or life planner that you may revisit to update and or make notes on your progress. Over time, your newly outlined response will become your default response. An accountability circle in the form of friends, mentors, and family with whom we can be vulnerable rewards us with a chance to share failures and successes at the same time. Being stuck on talking about our big moments alone negates growth. Sharing our failure, pain and shame builds self-mastery, coping skills, and positive mental dialogue.

Growth Mindset

> *My mission, should I choose to accept it, is to find peace with exactly who and what I am. To take pride in my thoughts, my appearance, my talents, my flaws and to stop this incessant worrying that I can't be loved as I am.*

Anaïs Nin, c.1966

At the heart of a growth mindset is the commitment to loving oneself as one is, at any point in time (and at all times, really), rather than waiting to love the future person that one may become. It is easy, after defining purpose, pursuit, and destination, after finding role models and icons, to subconsciously invalidate who we already are, thus failing to affirm our sufficiency right at this moment, at any moment. This can often lead to frustration, an inability to celebrate current victories, and low esteem. When we live by the fear that we are not enough, we are unable to align with the value that we already bring while yet committing to growth. This often leads to missed opportunities and low self-efficacy which I defined in an earlier chapter as a lack of belief in our ability to accomplish and surmount challenges. Rather than being stumped on how far ahead our big dreams look to us, how little we know, and how insufficient our current resumes, personalities, and skills are, there is a freedom to thrive in embracing a growth mindset.

> *I've seen so many people with this one consuming goal of proving themselves— in the classroom, in their careers, and in their relationships. Every situation calls for a confirmation of their intelligence, personality, or character. Every situation is evaluated: Will I succeed or fail? Will I look smart or dumb? Will I be accepted or rejected? Will I feel like a winner or a loser?*
>
> *There's another mindset in which these traits are not simply a hand you're dealt and have to live with, always trying to convince yourself and others that you have a royal flush when you're secretly worried it's a pair of tens. In this mindset, the hand you're dealt is just the starting point for development. This growth mindset is based on the belief that your basic qualities are things you can cultivate through your efforts.*[30]

Carol Dweck, 2022

After studying the behaviour of thousands of children, Carol Dweck coined the terms *fixed mindset* and *growth mindset* to describe the underlying beliefs people have about learning and intelligence. In her 2016 *Harvard Business Review* article titled 'What Having a "Growth Mindset' Actually Means"' she shared insights on how beliefs impact success. "… Individuals who believe their talents can be developed (through hard work, good strategies, and input from others) have a growth mindset. They tend to achieve more than those with a more fixed mindset (those who believe their talents are innate gifts). This is because they worry less about looking smart and they put more energy

---

[30] Carol Dweck, 'A Summary of Growth and Fixed Mindsets', Farnam Street Media (2022), https://fs.blog/carol-dweck-mindset/

into learning.[31] Relying on her work, Mindset Works (a growth mindset developing organisation) she states, "When students believe they can get smarter, they understand that effort makes them stronger. Therefore, they put in extra time and effort, and that leads to higher achievement."[32]

Going further to categorise the two mindsets and their characteristics, fixed mindset, which is characterised by a belief that intelligence is static, results in a tendency to avoid challenges, give up easily, see effort as fruitless, ignore useful negative feedback, and feel threatened by the success of others. Growth mindset on the other hand is characterised by a desire to learn, embrace challenges, persist in the face of setbacks, see effort as a path to mastery, learn from criticism, and find lessons/inspiration from the success of others.

Inspiration

Being inspired is at the heart of ageing backwards. It is a commitment to growing without constraints and dogma about where or what we should have arrived at or achieved. It is a refusal to be, and an insistence on becoming. It is the willingness to keep an open mind and see new perspectives on the things we already know a lot about, and the things that we know little about. At the initial stages of our lives, we are actively encouraged to grow, imagine, see the world, and rise to purpose. The inspiration behind the design of our early education and parenting dims as we go through the maturity stages of life.

---

[31] Carol Dweck, 'What Having a "Growth Mindset" Actually Means', *Harvard Business Review* (13 January 2016), https://hbr.org/2016/01/what-having-a-growth-mindset-actually-means

[32] Mindset Works, 'Dr. Dweck's Research into Growth Mindset Changed Education Forever', (2017), https://www.mindsetworks.com/science/

As we mature, attainment shapes into a select and tunnelled perspective. We race toward milestones and often do so at the expense of parts of our soul that we no longer have the time to nurture. It is not uncommon to then arrive at pinnacles, and yet feel a sense of emptiness. A friend with whom I celebrated the purchase of his dream car once told me that he lost his excitement after the first drive. What causes us to suddenly feel empty when we achieve something that was once a faraway dream? What is it that drives us to, like addicts, continually seek new *highs* in a new car, house, or possession that will give us a fresh dose of anticipation, exhilaration, and fulfilment? The answer is in how we define purpose and attainment. When our reason for being encapsulates more than material gain, we rise to a life filled with attainment.

Inspiration and purposefulness are as crucial to happiness in the maturity stages of life as they are in childhood. When we fail to feed our curiosity, inspiration, and purpose, our souls become bored and accustomed. Our mental pictures no longer excite us. We begin to go through the motions, counting down till the end of life. That is not the life we were designed for – *a life of resistance.*

When we advance without resistance, we become open. The doors we keep locked, the people we choose not to see, and the values we choose not to consider begin to find meaning. The tendency is for us to then develop respect for the things we do not understand and even for the things we do not want to know or understand. In advancing without resistance, we tap into a new level of empathy. The more we embrace this lifelong learning approach, the more we permit others to grow. People's foolishness no longer grates, at least not as much, we are foolish too, so we do not mind. We begin to tap into our natural role as channels and connectors. We become less self-absorbed and more other-focused. Our desire to be there for others and support them through life makes a radical shift. To become a channel is to become light – to provide the necessary guidance and yet give up the fight for the spotlight. When we become a channel for others, we rise to a higher calling that is characterised by less war with self, less judgement, less competition, and more embracing. Our circle of influence begins to expand.

You do feel yourself ageing backwards right in your bones when you embrace *life without resistance*. I felt it when I broke free of limiting beliefs. I let go of ideas about who or where I was supposed to be or how wise and attaining my station in life should look. I simply permitted myself to live for new hope, an assuredness that life is not over, a willingness to be utterly foolish. It does feel like a reversal. The exact phrase that I use – *ageing backwards*.

Further Reading

Eve Lackman, 'Ikigai [Classic]', Creately (2022), https://creately.com/diagram/example/imjlltqm2/ikigai-%5Bclassic%5D

Jeffery Gaines, Ph.D, 'The Philosophy of Ikigai: 3 Examples About Finding Purpose', Positive Psychology (2022), https://positivepsychology.com/ikigai/

Resources

The Ikigai Template, Recalibrate How You Spend Your Time, (2022), https://docs.google.com/presentation/d/1YhbZ-

Who Am I?

xcmcgMqO4FbRgsOstoqGFDJoO9yGYCMKzoJwAY/edit#slide=id.g5c6d29a368_2_8

Chapter 5

Let's Get to Work

Stories are powerful, they are part of the fabric of life and meaning because they serve as a medium of imagination and communication. Whatever the medium through which stories are told – the written word, spoken word, motion picture – stories have been with us since ancient times. Many of us can remember line-by-line quotes from our best movies. Others with graphic recall may remember faces, body language, and scenes, enough to go back in time and even re-enact history.

Dr. Jaron Jones, described the role of self-narratives also called self-stories in his TEDxUF talk. In his speech, he shared the story of his Black friend's response to the police, a response that was based on stereotypes about policing in the Black-American community. He described his friend's response as "someone else writing his friend's narrative that wasn't a reflection of him" and credited his friends action to an oversaturation of rap music and media with racist biases.

The stories we tell ourselves about ourselves are our identity. When we fail to tell our own stories, someone else tells them for us, and to us, and our lives become someone's will and imagination. In the earlier chapter, I highlighted the importance of defining identity, one that ensures we live a life of consciousness and attainment. In this chapter, we explore essential life tools that help to define purpose and identity, in essence a storytelling toolkit for personal attainment.

Obituary Exercise

One of the greatest storytelling tools of life is an obituary. The writer attempts to condense the deceased's life into milestones and snippets. A well-written obituary might make the reader feel a connection to the departed just by the anecdotes or shared experiences in it. I first encountered the obituary exercise during my undergraduate days and to date, I remember sketches of the story that I wrote about myself. I simply wrote what I willed to happen in my future and what I wanted to be known for. At certain key inflection points in my career, more than 10 years after, I recall that I did write them, even when I had no idea how they would come to be. A classic obituary is a third-person narrative about someone after their demise.

This exercise on the other hand is a personal obituary, written by yourself. You may think of it as an opportunity to write at your current age what you will like to be written about you and the end of your life..

The obituary exercise prompts one to dialogue with self; it teaches one to capture the big things that will happen in our lives and then get a chance to ponder on the steps to becoming the person we have presented ourselves with. Consider it as a way of introducing self to self. It is not a life plan or goals tracker. Its tone can be range from formal to informal based on the writer's preference. It is an obituary in every sense of the word and should be written in the past, not present tense. There are no real rules about what you may include in this exercise, I have provided a guide below to get you started.

1. Start with a highlight of your personality. Consider including the things you like the most about yourself (your values, your quirks, your purpose, preferences, skills etc.) and the capabilities you are currently building and expect to have developed expertise for by the end of your life. For the longest time, I have introduced myself by my love for high life music, my attraction to Igbo men (an ethnic group in Nigeria), and my love for maximalist fashion.

2. In your second paragraph, write about the key goals and milestones you will have accomplished in your lifetime (you may include timelines). Include goals that seem unattainable. Imagine that you could have any life you want and write what that life would have looked like. Include what you may consider as serious goals/ dreams, but also include the ones that you do not necessarily think are serious-minded. If you like them, include them. This is not a contest of your big wins; it is simply your obituary.

3. Finally in your fourth paragraph write about the impact you would have made on the world and the lives of those who matter to you.

The most important success factor for this exercise is vulnerability. Your obituary should be recognisable to you, it is not a chance to write about one's favourite role model, it is an intimate portrayal of the life story that you want to be told about you when your time on earth is done. When you read your obituary, you make connections to who you are. Right at that moment, clarity on what you should spend your time doing emerges, and you begin to make associations and connections from where you are to where you want to be. It answers the *who am I* question in a way that few other short exercises can.

Izin was a saleswoman turned politician who taught a model of change that enabled people all over the world who had dealt with life traumas to find healing and purpose through life-transforming insights and wellness practices. In her later years, she travelled globally teaching wellness, spirituality and studying the world's religions.

Known for her humour, obsession with her favourite person on earth, - her mother, and her multidisciplinary skills, she led innovative creative and digital companies for several decades and was well recognised in the global business and impact communities.

She enjoyed travelling and lived on five continents at different points in her life.

Izin is survived by her a large family of children, grandchildren and great-grandchildren, **and a global family of** lifelong **learners.**

Figure 5.1 **Snippet of A hypothetical obituary**

Ikigai Exercise

Ikigai is a purpose model popularised by Dan Buettner's expose on the Okinawa community in Japan, whose residents, amongst the longest living on earth, combine healthy diets with a lifestyle that is built on purpose – *the reason for being.* He posits that "Older Okinawans can readily articulate the reason they get up in the morning. Their purpose-imbued lives give them clear roles of responsibility and feelings of being needed well into their 100s."[33]

Laura Oliver, writing for the World Economic Forum, says about ikigai:

> *While there is no direct English translation, ikigai is thought to combine the Japanese words ikiru, meaning to live, and kai, meaning the realization of what one hopes for. Together these definitions create the concept of a reason to live or the idea of having a purpose in life.*[34]

Laura Oliver, 2017

The model that I share simply extends storytelling into an already powerful purpose model. Ikigai shows us how to answer questions about the details of our life in the present, and connect our answers to purpose. Some people go as far as building more than one ikigai framework to consider different scenarios and possibilities. My practice is to use it as a holistic purpose tool capturing a range of purposes. Two

[33] Dan Buettner, 'These People Live Longer Than Anyone. Here are 9 Things They Do', Mind Body Green (2014), https://www.mindbodygreen.com/0-14305/these-people-live-longer-than-anyone-here-are-9-things-they-do.html

[34] Laura Oliver, 'Is This Japanese Concept the Secret to a Long, Happy, Meaningful Life?' World Economic Forum (9 August 2017), https://www.weforum.org/agenda/2017/08/is-this-japanese-concept-the-secret-to-a-long-life/

models of ikigai exist in the world today, one that anchors ikigai to monetary success and another that emphasises its use as a values-based tool for purposeful living. I see room for the use of one ikigai model for both monetary and values-based pursuits. In my personal practice, I tell multiple stories through one ikigai matrix. In these multiple stories, I create pictures of several potential futures that have personal meaning; I write them and keep refining them year in and out. In my version, I highlight multiple future possibilities, not one ultimate goal. This is likely because I do not believe in an ultimate. I believe instead that several multiple states of happiness and successes abound, and that is how I approach the ikigai.

The model pictured below depicts that the ikigai is a point of intersection, a confluence of our most valuable attributes.

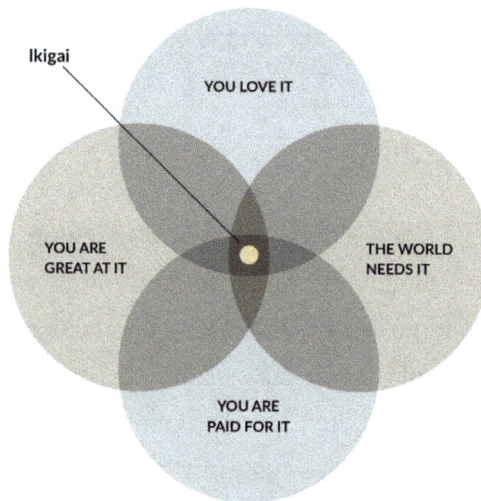

Figure 5.2 **The Ikigai Model, adapted from Positive Psychology's Toolkit, 2020** [35]

---

[35] Adapted from Positive Psychology Toolkit (2020), https://positivepsychology.com/ikigai/

Figure 5.3 **Find Your Ikigai, Bodetree, adapted from Francesc Miralles** .[36]

How To Build Your Ikigai Model

The first thing in developing your model is to find multiple sheets of plain paper if you prefer to do it by hand, or an e-spreadsheet that allows you to make multiple notes that you bring back together into the model. The ikigai checklist is built on four question pillars.

- What am I good at?
- What can I be paid for?

---

[36] Chris Myers, 'How To Find Your Ikigai and Transform Your Outlook On Life and Business', Forbes (23 February 2018), https://www.forbes.com/sites/chrismyers/2018/02/23/how-to-find-your-ikigai-and-transform-your-outlook-on-life-and-business/?sh=75d350002ed4

- What do I love?
- What does the world need?

As seen in the model, each circle intersects to give meaning.

Follow the steps below:

- Step 1: Generate as many responses to the question prompt as possible.
- Step 2: Fill them into the sub-segments that they belong. (passion, mission, vocation, and profession)
- Step 3: Identify which of your responses combines passion, mission, vocation, and profession. Those go into the central spot in your ikigai map.

Example

In this example, I show the storytelling version of a writer's ikigai

1. What am I good at? **Writing**
2. What can I be paid for? **Digital content, books, research writing, media writing, journalism**
3. What do I love? **Teaching**
4. What does the world need? **Diversity researchers? – think of this as stretch goals, or new opportunities emerging in the world that you may not have capabilities for.**

Below is the completed ikigai.

	Zone A	Zone B	Zone C	Zone D	Zone E
MY IKIGAI WORKSHEET	Ikigai	Profession	Mission	Passion	Vocation
	Self-actualisation tied to monetary gains	Comfort without passion	Joy, may not lead to money	Satisfaction – no social acceptance, lack of validation	Uncertainty
	Career Validation Zone		A map of possibilities and purposes		
	Helps situate yourself and find meaning in the world of work. Work means more than just a paycheck.		Rewards may or may not be monetary at the moment. Mission and passion bring affirmation, community, gifts, and uniqueness. These are already forms of self-actualisation		

A Picture of Possible Futures

Role/ Title	Sweet Spot	Profession	Mission	Passion	Vocation
Name it the role or title)	Digital Journalist	Content, digital, multimedia journalism	Teaching visually impaired children	Visually impaired alternative learning, handmade dance craft, voice-over mimics	Diversity journalism
Where will it/does it exist?	Multiple locations	Online	Homes, schools, shelters	Sign language institutes, government-funded research	Remote

				and innovation centres	
Where is it located? (companies)	Facebook, National Geographic, Google		Dallas Learning Center	Self-owned learning research company	Diversity journalism
What will I focus on now?	Getting into management at Google for 3 years		Volunteering at a non-profit	Join pitch contests and fellowships on language innovation	A short course on diversity journalism to see if I like it

Personal Narrative
I am a visually impaired learning researcher; I write digital stories at a people-centred technology company. I enjoy dancing and I volunteer at the Dallas Learning Center.
I dance and mimic voice-overs, enjoy writing digital stories at Google, while building the future of alternative learning for the visually impaired.

Figure 5.4 **A hypothetical ikigai example**

You will notice that in this example, several portions of the writer's ikigai are left blank. You do not have to populate all sections of the model. Use it to answer questions that you can relate to and then tell yourself the stories of your future by connecting the dots all the way to the responses in your obituary exercise.

The obituary and ikigai exercises are powerful life tools that support a continuous personal growth practice. As a system of questioning, journaling, and purpose planning, they catalyse growth through self-assessment, inspiration, brainstorming, and personal stories. Think of the obituary as an opening story into one's dreams and possibilities, and the outcome of your ikigai as the closing story, always a work in progress. It is a live document that keeps one grounded and inspired, underscored by a commitment to questioning, vulnerability, and self-inspiration.

Chapter 6

Science of Silence

A life filled with connections is a good life. A life filled with
noise is a stressed one.

Sound is a natural life occurrence. All human forms use sound as a
means of expression. Birds, sea animals, and even plants have their
variation of sound. But sound in excess? Like all other life forms,
humans suffer from noise pollution in many ways. Sound, sight, and
words are needed in balance. An excess of any results in disharmony
and affects our ability to thrive.

Zen Buddhism

Zen Buddhism is a life practice that I cannot speak of with much
authority. I have neither studied nor practiced it sufficiently to make
any claims. My experience of Zen Buddhism is limited to yoga
practices that incorporate stillness, exercise, and silent music – sounds.
At the time of my yoga indoctrination, I was not seeking to understand
Buddhism. I simply took a free yoga class at a family gym when I visited

friends in San Francisco back in 2017. I fell in love. The movements and music suited me. The music was reminiscent of my worship practice back home in Nigeria. Christian music can be safely divided into two genres – praise and worship. Some Christians like myself have a distinct preference, others do not. I am a worship addict. Simply put, I thrive in the silence of quiet music, and it is my cure-all for life. Sadness, happiness, and conflict, all find healing in it.

The following are some insights into Zen Buddhism:

> *Silence in Japan is traditionally associated with truthfulness. This belief derives from Zen Buddhism ... According to Zen Buddhism, enlightenment can be reached only through silence and teachings can only be understood with silent meditation and contemplation.*[37]

Sara Bortoluz, 2016

> *The practice is meditation. 'Sitting Zen' (Japanese: zazen) has always been central to Zen training centers, where monks rise early each morning for meditation practice and do long retreats consisting of many, many silent unmoving hours on the cushion.*
>
> *What is Zazen? It literally means 'sitting Zen.' Put simply, it's 'seated meditation' as done in the Zen style — upright in good posture, paying careful attention to breathing in your belly until you are fully alert and present.*[38]

Norman Fischer, 2017

---

[37] Sara Bortoluz, 'The Hidden Meaning of Silence—Insights From Japanese Buddhist Culture', Elephant Journal (5 July 2016), https://www.elephantjournal.com/2016/07/the-hidden-meaning-of-silence-insights-from-japanese-buddhist-culture/

[38] Norman Fischer, 'What is Zen Buddhism and How Do You Practice It?', Lion's Roar (13 December 2017), https://www.lionsroar.com/what-is-zen-buddhism-and-how-do-you-practice-it/

> *Zen sends us looking inside us for enlightenment. There's no need to search outside ourselves for the answers; we can find the answers in the same place that we found the questions. ... The essence of Zen Buddhism is achieving enlightenment by seeing one's original mind (or original nature) directly; without the intervention of the intellect.*[39]

BBC, 2002

As an introverted child, I spent a lot of time in my own company and in the company of books, so much so that my mother thought that I might be socially awkward. She was correct. My imagination was filled with words. In real life, I used words so infrequently that when faced with the need to use them, I stuttered and stumbled in extreme shyness. I found my voice later, and when I did, I filled my life with a lot of words and a lot of busyness. When I began to reassess my life at the pinnacle of an identity crisis which I discussed in the earlier chapters, I made my way back to solitude. When my mental battles became overwhelming, when shock and sadness became my every waking day, I sought a safe space without sound, without television or screen, and there I would hear myself speak in silence and hear silence speak to me. Today, I have a mastery of solitude that combines curated spaces with music – only when I feel like music, personal reflection – and specific times of the day (stillness of my mornings, bathing rituals, sleeping rituals, music rituals, etc.) to unlock, clarity, peace, creativity, and mastery. This is the science that I share on the following pages.

---

[39] BBC, 'Zen Buddhism', (2002),
https://www.bbc.co.uk/religion/religions/buddhism/subdivisions/zen_1.shtml

Art, Science

An art, A science
A mantra, A chant
A song of silence
A cure for madness

...

Science of silence
Alone yet a many
Healing and refining
Making whole yet breaking
Questions and answers, questions and answers
A cure for madness

...

Science of silence
In notes and in words,
time to write them
The holy grail of your making
Here, a note on acceptance, There a note on forgiveness
Here a note on craft, There a note on why
A cure for madness

....

Science of silence
A design in aloneness

...

For one lifetime, and many more
A place for a lifetime
A cure for madness

> *Our culture made a virtue of living only as extroverts. We discouraged the inner journey, the quest for a center. So we lost our center and have to find it again.*[40]

Annais Nin, c.1966

It is no coincidence that the art of writing is often spoken of as an endeavour untaken in silence. Like many other creative endeavours, in silence, words and life forms begin to tell their meaning and show the writer the path to completion. The science of silence is a solitude practice that I recommend based on its immense value to my healing and my belief in its potency as a tool for the self-awareness and identity-building practices that I have shared in the previous chapters. Simply put, the journey to self-definition is as much one that requires engagement with the external world, as it is one that requires time spent with oneself in meditation. In psychology, religious worship, and across cultures, silence is studied and adopted to enhance quality of life. Zen Buddhism, the Japanese meditation practice is a way of life that is incorporated into wellness practices across the world, and for good reason. While the exercises that I shared in earlier chapters arm us with life planning tools, aimed at building a clear set of purposeful inspirations and ideologies about who we are, solitude remains the processing place for those tools.

In solitude, our personal stories take on meaning and we can immerse in them, (meditate), query them and understand them, ultimately understanding who we are. Solitude is the place where we refine, reaffirm, deduce, and validate our being. Like a loop, we write our

---

[40] Goalcast, '24 Eye-Opening Anais Nin Quotes to Inspire Deeper Living', (2002), https://www.goalcast.com/anais-nin-quotes-inspire-deeper-living/

stories, define our purposes, and then, we meditate, clarify, validate, and tell more stories. We go about day-to-day living, bring back insights, edit our personal stories, and on and on, in a practice of self-discovery and personal growth.

To master silence, one must practice silence. There is really no other magical way to learn of its immense value than to find time for silence. Through retreats and deliberate daily rituals of life, we may learn mastery of solitude that rewards with a rich life.

Here are some thoughts to bear in mind for mastering silence:

1. Make time weekly for time spent alone. Decide what day or timeframe you will allocate to being quietly on your own without any interference

2. Cultivated Atmosphere: A cultivated atmosphere is a big part of stillness practices. For some, the silence of their bedroom is enough, others seek wide open spaces, walk parks, waterfronts, etc. It is hard to practice silence in the company of loud sounds and loud forms. Choose locations that give you a sense of calmness and peace.

3. Peak Moments: I learned about the concept of *peak moments* through a Christian teaching on innovation that encouraged time spent cataloguing the moments when you suddenly feel inspired or sense new ideas or solutions to existing problems. The teaching suggested that we became conscious of our thoughts during our alone moments (waking moments, shower moments – specifically shower, not bucket baths, moments handling laundry or washing cookery, time exercising etc.), essentially, moments of the day where we are left with our

thoughts. According to the teaching, over time, as you catalogue those moments, you notice a trend of specific times of day or personal activities that lead to creativity, new ideas and inspiration. I have found this teaching to be correct. Peak moments for some are moments of one's day when the mind is least loaded. For others, it may simply be multiple moments of the day when they find the time to be alone undertaking some activity or the other.

4. Journaling: Keep a tablet or notepad and pen within easy reach. Take notes of new ideas or thoughts that may be transferred or revisited during a life planning session. Over time, you will connect your thoughts and inspiration to lifetime interests and sometimes mundane everyday concerns. Journaling was highlighted in the previous chapter an ongoing practise leveraging personal planning tools. Maintaining a bedside journal is a way to consistently capture one's thoughts and information flow during silence practices. Words which in the future can be used to develop phrases, ideas or quotes to contribute to one's affirmation practise or simply find use in other aspects of life.

5. Silence Music: The life and clarity that comes to us in solitude, in aloneness, is profound and touches on anything at all that we may be involved with. It is a practice that can guide us to healing through affirming thoughts, affirming dialogue, and affirming music – both those with words and those with just sound. On repeat, silence music becomes a chant, a mantra that we subconsciously recite in our silent moments. In a sense, giving ourselves power by feeding off self and words that carry power. I describe this experience as a cure for madness. Our

minds are fed with all sorts of madness daily. Affirming silence music is a way to reengineer the words and thoughts that we internalise to the point where we subconsciously begin to act in tandem with them

Personal Mantras: In the practice of journaling, we emerge with statements about ourselves. Those statements can be purpose statements, claims, affirmations or dreams.

6. Mantras can easily be considered frivolous and religious rather than what they really are, a practical powerful affirmation practice. We all are inspired by words, words we see, words we hear in a line of music, quotes, etc. Mantras or repeated words and quotes about oneself or certain circumstances, behaviour, or life perspective can be incorporated into a daily silence practice to foster self-belief, healing, inspiration, or break addictions. It is not frivolous to build or adopt a set of words that hold profound personal meaning into daily practice. It is in fact practical to do so. By memorising and speaking those words, we reaffirm them, we reaffirm what they mean to us, and give ourselves the power to be what those words inspire us to be.

Have you ever felt the onset of madness?
Have you ever felt something breaking?
Not bones or stoneware, but mind and spirit
Seek the science of silence,
A cure for madness.

In the introduction to this book, I wrote about my single years, the years and moments of observation and questioning. Years where I was simply available to be around my mother and watch her being her. I alluded to the impact of those years on this book. I do not think I would have written this book if I didn't have the gift of solitude. Time with mother, then time alone, to think, to google something, mention it to a friend randomly, ponder some more, and finally decide how to go forward with it. Silence in that season showed me what I needed to see even when I did not know it.

In solitude, I looked at my own sexuality. I simply just looked at it and asked why? what? and where do I go from here? I knew, in silence, to let go, to simply breathe and let the unheard pain of my past abuse go. I also learned that I was not as keen on sex as I had begun to think that I should be. At this time, most of my friends had healthy, sexual relationships, I had thought that it was necessary, that I was odd not to do the same. In solitude, I knew that I would not. I knew that for that season, sex which meant more to me now, which I could now indulge, was yet less urgent. It could wait. Despite that I had decided against a version of identity that defines a woman by her sexual repression, which forces her to hide her sexuality, I knew that liberation for me, did not mean indulgence. Not at that time. I was finally sexually liberated, acknowledging my own desires, yet conscious that in that season, I would not indulge.

My solitude moments are in the early hours of dawn when I'm barely awake. Disparate thoughts come into clear cohesion, new ideas drop on my mind as I indulge most mornings in an hour or more of silence. I often start the day by taking notes on my phone to ensure I do not lose the thoughts and clarity of those moments. I once listened to a free message on Mindvalley.com, an educational website that publishes content for personal and spiritual development. Though I do not recall the name of the teacher, he encouraged waking up one hour earlier than one needed to and to meditate during that hour. This is where I adopted the one-hour morning rule, and it has been rewarding. Many of the ideas I've happened on and refined have been in those moments, between bed and bath rituals.

Solitude vs. Isolation

Time spent in meditation is an active choice to indulge in rewarding life practice. Isolation on the other hand is a subconscious withdrawal that we have no real control over. The mind may wander aimless, unable to form or hold unto coherent thought. Seek help and speak to someone if you are struggling with isolation. Silence practice and isolation are completely different.

Chapter 7

All About Maya

My first real introduction to Maya Angelou was after her death, through *And Still I Rise,* a post-humous documentary made in her honour.[41] In the documentary, Maya, who was a poet, writer, and dancer, was referred to as "a redwood tree, with deep roots in American culture". According to Jessie Szalay, "… California redwoods (also called coast redwoods) are nature's skyscrapers. …These giants can live to be 2,000 years old and have graced the planet for more than 240 million years. Though they once thrived throughout much of the Northern Hemisphere, today redwoods are only found on the coast from central California through southern Oregon."[42]

I have taken the time to stew on Maya's legacy, with the intent to understand why the world seemed to stand still at her passing, and why she had been dubbed after the oldest tree in the world. I found that

[41] Apple TV, 'And Still I Rise', (2016), https://tv.apple.com/us/movie/maya-angelou-and-still-i-rise/umc.cmc.16jkjby8fjjtkwk46fbs7eumj

[42] Jessie Szalay, 'Giant Sequoias and Redwoods: The Largest and Tallest Trees', Live Science (5 May 2017), https://www.livescience.com/39461-sequoias-redwood-trees.html

Maya had an amazing gift for storytelling. Through autobiographies about her own life written between 1969 and 2013, she connected people to their own experiences and realities. Many accounts in the documentary, both male and female, identified themselves in Maya's books. One commentator highlighted how Maya's uncanny observational skill, recall, and vulnerability connected her personal stories to other people's realities, enabling them to find the words for emotions and experiences that they previously had no way to express.

In the later part of her life, Maya became one of the icons of the American Civil Rights Movement, a custodian of the history and cultural evolution of the Black-American Race. She could do that because, throughout her adult life, she chose to represent and act what she believed. There was honesty and vulnerability in the books she wrote. She shared the good, the bad, and the ugly. Maya's identity was unambiguous. She chose her Blackness over all else: her fashion, hair, community, and message, were tied to this identity, and she became the stimulus for several Black Americans to explore and understand their roots.

A values-based identity is how I describe Maya's. She simply chose to be her values, and that choice was reflected in her lifestyle until her death. I first used values-defining tools in a personality assessment test some years back, but I have not referred to them in the past few years as I have further embraced my own identity. My experience is that the more one engages life based on clearly identified values, the easier it is to abide by what one stands for. Over time, it becomes second nature to make choices that align with those values.

Value maps provide the right words to capture one's essence unambiguously. They can be a solid starting point to exploring what values mean to you, what you most closely align with, and where to begin the journey to a personal system of self-checks that over time become fully immersed. One of the things that a value map has done for me is that it has given me the courage to be different. In situations where before, I might have struggled with words or even my position on a subject, becoming closely attuned with my values has made it easier to navigate unfamiliar territories.

The VIA Institute of Character's character strengths classification which I have captured below is a good way to start the journey to identifying or reaffirming one's values. They offer a free survey on their website and multiple resources that you may use to define and continually refine your values.[43] In addition to clarity, authenticity, and autonomy in decision making, defining values (character strengths according to VIA Institute) is a way to affirm oneself and enhance the quality of one's mental dialogue. By answering the question, why does this value matter to me? we find a place for them in our history and day-to-day living.

[43] VIA Institute, 'The VIA Character Strengths Survey', (2022) https://www.viacharacter.org/survey/account/register

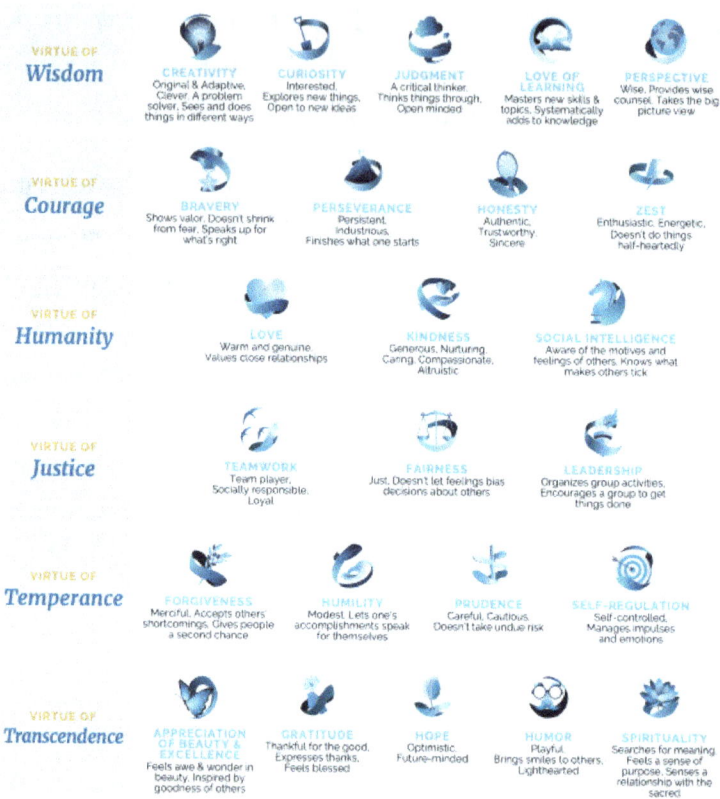

Figure 7.1 **VIA Character Classification**

Character in Action

One of the most empowering ways to navigate or strengthen one's perspective is to take action. Sometimes that action simply means speaking up as often as possible, sharing one's perspective, and teaching alternative approaches. There is immense power in giving voice to the convictions that we live by, and connecting with movements and communities that embody our values is a great way to do so. It is stifling to believe in big things, to be motivated, yet stuck trying to do these things all by oneself. By joining a community or cause, we reaffirm and validate our perspective through collective action. That is not all that we stand to gain, we also begin to deepen our understanding of the values that we have embraced. We may even decide against them, and that is just fine. That in itself is the value of action.

When I started volunteering in the areas where I felt compelled to, I realised that I didn't know much about them. Volunteering forced me to ask a whole other set of questions, listen to other perspectives, investigate solutions that existed in other parts of the world, and imagine how those solutions might be adapted in my community. As with every formal and informal skill that we learn in life, to navigate culture and identity, we must activate our interests and perspectives. It is only by doing so, that we come to a full appreciation of our own beliefs, connect with a potential community of people who hold similar views, and begin to shape a circle of influence that is more attuned. In essence, our circle becomes more deliberate and affirming. I have found these types of connections to be by far some of the most rewarding experiences of my life. Meeting people who think alike, and who may then partner with us to make an influence is immensely rewarding and provides a positive ecosystem for growth.

A Healthy Perspective of Honour, Shame, and Boundaries

A good portion of this book has highlighted culture's role in shaping our perspectives and therefore, our identity and attainment. I have also shared practices and tools that help to build an independent purpose-led viewpoint. However, we do not live in isolation. We must navigate the day-to-day opportunities and challenges that come with living in a world where perspectives differ and change often. Navigating personal preferences and acceptable rules takes consciousness.

Honour has many applications but for this book, I will define honour by one of its close synonyms, *morals*. According to Oxford English Dictionary, *morals* are "concerned with or derived from the code of interpersonal behaviour that is considered right or acceptable in a particular society.".[44] A healthy perspective of honour, as a code of behaviour is arrived at by channelling acceptable codes through the fire of values. Does code A match value B? does code C match value D? and on and on. Essentially, a healthy code of honour is built on the back of a healthy code of values. When values take precedence over history, and doctrine, we can make choices that move us forward as individuals and as a collective. Understanding honour, as a function of values, is what gives us the right perspective on shame and boundaries. Values are the underlying thread that validates or invalidates honour, shame, loss of esteem, and boundaries.

Guilt and shame are feelings we all navigate through our lives; we are bound to make mistakes, and even act in shameful manners. The inevitability of humanity is that we are all flawed and not infallible.

---

[44] https://www.oed.com

However, when we do feel guilty or ashamed, where we go from those feelings should anchor on something more than *what people will say* or *how it looks,* in essence, biases. Instead, a values-based approach inspires us to assess our feelings in a healthy, affirming manner. It gives us the freedom to take responsibility where we have erred, but in a manner that is free of toxic self-dialogue and labels. By aligning clearly with an underlying code of values, we become free to thrive, even in situations when our positions or outcomes do not necessarily match people's labels or stereotypes about who and what we should look like.

Unconscious Bias

To have a healthy perspective of honour and boundaries, we must understand the role of unconscious biases and commit to thinking through our actions and inactions by querying them on the merit of values.

> *Unconscious biases are social stereotypes about certain groups of people that individuals form outside their own conscious awareness. Everyone holds unconscious beliefs about various social and identity groups, and these biases stem from one's tendency to organize social worlds by categorizing. Unconscious bias is far more prevalent than conscious prejudice and often incompatible with one's conscious values.[45]*

University of California San Francisco, Office of Diversity and Outreach, 2022

---

[45] University of California Office of Diversity and Outreach, Unconscious Bias Training (2022), https://diversity.ucsf.edu/programs-resources/training/unconscious-bias-training#:~:text=Unconscious%20biases%20are%20social%20stereotypes,organize%20social%20worlds%20by%20categorizing

In the earlier part of this book, I wrote about my experience with unconscious bias, how I went from feeling unhappy about stereotypes towards my family to becoming judgemental about blended families, amongst other personal beliefs that I internalised about myself which were completely different from the rules that I consciously thought I was living my life by. When social labels and unconscious biases pull us in one direction, clearly defined values help us move toward appropriate humane choices and actions.

Empathy and Root Causes

When we approach people and our differences with an intent to understand, we often lead the way for real change. Listening consciously with the intent to learn prepares us to navigate differences with positive outcomes. Leading with empathy, compels us to be less insistent on enforcing our perspective and be more curious to know what is behind another. When we lead with empathy, we understand the role of varied life experiences and the selectiveness and subjectiveness of enlightenment. When we listen consciously, we empathise and become more inclusive; that enables us to live in harmony with community and with self. Understanding that behaviours are merely symptoms of an underlying belief system – in essence, a reflection of our roots – curbs the hastiness to judge which we are all susceptible to.

Conclusion

We gain fresh consciousness at different inflection points. Though rebirths happen through all stages of our lives, as we encounter new knowledge, experiences, and milestones, there are pivotal moments when we affirm identity, when we simply determine that we have chosen to be a certain type for the rest of our lives.

It is somewhat odd to describe humans in all our multiple roles and exploits as being summed into one. Yes, we remain in multiple and in constant flux, yet there does come a time when for those who are fortunate to get there, we firmly acknowledge identity. For those who do, their life takes an even deeper meaning. They have a clear concept of self, they accept who they are – good, bad, or ugly – and build a life from there on. Attaining personal consciousness is not about becoming an adult, even though in a way, it is a form of adulting. It is more about knowing oneself enough to be in alignment with one's *reason for being*.

Identity signals such as race, language, religious practice, marital status, and language, are not bad things in themselves. Words do exist as a means of communicating and categorising; being able to define oneself beyond the classic identity constructs is a chance to be deeply interested in the best life that one can have. Navigating life's complexities, recovering from failure and trauma, and loving in a healthy manner, all depend on our internal radar and convictions which are enhanced by our life and growth practices. Though biases may continue till infinity, affirming life practices ensure that we find our place, our collective, and attainment in this world.

There is no other planet, at least not at the moment. Outliers will exist right here along with those who fit in perfectly. Each must seek his or her harmony and the opportunity to live their best lives within the window of opportunity that we all have. I hope that collectively, humanity embraces the demand for consciousness; that we build a way of living, a value system that hungers for clarity and growth beyond the boundaries of laid down doctrine. I hope that we all become brave and unlock our fears, both of self in our communities, and of otherness. You do not need anyone's permission to be here. Give yourself the wings to fly and go right ahead!

www.ingramcontent.com/pod-product-compliance
Lightning Source LLC
LaVergne TN
LVHW021122080426
835513LV00011B/1200